THE 21ST CENTURY

HIP-HOP
MINSTREL SHOW

ARE WE CONTINUING THE
BLACKFACE TRADITION?

RAPHAEL HEAGGANS

University Readers™
San Diego, CA

First published in the United States of America in 2009 by University Readers

Cover design by Monica Hui Hekman

13 12 11 10 09   1 2 3 4 5

Printed in the United States of America

ISBN: 978-1-934269-51-0

University Readers™
800.200.3908 I www.universityreaders.com

Contents

Acknowledgments

I am so thankful to God for His many blessings. Without Him, I am nothing. I have been through some tough times in my life, but I am grateful to Him for my family and loved ones who stood with me through the thick, thicker, and the thickest. It is part of my destiny to have written this book.

To my parents Joseph and Dorothy: You believed in me during times I did not believe in myself. It was through your prayers, love, and support that have made me the strong survivor that I am.

To my son Christopher: You are a dynamic young man who has consistently helped me to grow. You kept me cognizant that I must be the best father I have been called to be. You are the biggest blessing and inspiration in my life.

To my siblings: Gwendal, Joseph Jr., Christopher, Eric, Tammy, Marvin, Emily, Charles, and Corey: I appreciate your encouragement and support.

To Mary Brinson, Henrietta Greene, Derrick Fields, Ronald Dalton, Bishop Robert Taylor, Pastor Darius Pridgen: You were among the first to encourage me to write this book. I thank you for your insight, feedback, life lessons, encouragement, and support.

To Lisa LaBella: You have been a huge cheerleader of my work since I presented it at the National Association for Multicultural

Education conference. I am thankful for your support that helped give birth to this text.

To Belinda Bruce: I appreciate your vital editorial contribution and insight to this book.

Preface

A SPRINGBOARD FOR EXAMINING
HIP-HOP THROUGH A CRITICAL LENS¹

Do we seek to produce any more generations of African Americans who, regardless of any achievements they can personally claim, go on to produce more people who hate who they are?²

—*Katherine Bankole*

The alchemic ingredients of the recipe *Jim Crow's Hip-Hop Surprise* is quite simple. The objective of baking this recipe is to make a socially *unconscious*ⁱ hip-hop song or video. For starters, it must include several packages of breasts, hips,

---

i Socially unconscious hip-hop music is the opposite of conscious hip-hop music. Socially unconscious hip-hop music has themes of misogyny, oppression, drugs, pimping, sex, and other false portrayals of Black manhood and womanhood. Such music perpetuates stereotypes and distortions of Black people and does not uplift the masses. It does not focus on social justice and consciousness for all people. Socially conscious hip-hop music, much like rap music, has themes related to the social injustices among Blacks and Latinos, while still appealing to the masses and incorporating, fun, romance, and unity within it.

thighs, bitches, hos, and tricks, preferably well beaten physically, mentally, and/or spiritually; several cups of finely chopped *niggas*, and lightly beaten chickenheads; mix in slabs of sex, baggy pants, prisons, bling blings; then add blunts, ghettos, fine cars, spinners; then finally sprinkle it with a computer-generated beat. This recipe—unbeknownst to those White and Black youth who deem it a culinary experience to treasure—is filled with all-purpose dour specifically designed to enslave them psychologically.

Jim Crow's Hip-Hop Surprise is now the blueprint by which hip-hop is a job made to order for its Black hip-hop artists. These artists are given the recipe to keep the dollars heavily flowing in the pockets of the record companies they pay obeisance to. Part of the Black male hip-hop artist's servitude includes exuding lyrically and attitudinally patriarchal ways of thinking through lyrics and attitude that contradicts his history. He takes on the role of the oppressor by objectifying and dehumanizing women; he forgets how his ancestors were falsely imprisoned for trumped-up crimes, yet he celebrates prison culture in style, attitude, and nuance. His insouciant attitude helps him to disregard the Black and White youth who may mimic him by adopting his fashions and acting out scenes from his lyrics, not realizing the consequence.

Many of these artists often have fans, whether they are 5 or 35 years of age, eating out of their hands, reciting their in-your-face lyrics and imitating their styles and persona without knowing how to critique what they hear and see. This naiveté contributes to the mis-education of Whites and Blacks about the Black experience and Black history. But while the sauciness of socially unconscious hip-hop appears to leave a savory taste in the mouths of White and Black listeners who eat greedily from *Jim Crow's Hip-Hop Surprise,* these youth—with every swallow—intensify stereotypic perceptions of all things Black.

The challenges faced by our African ancestors[ii] and their triumphs over various forms of oppression are forgotten or un-acknowledged in unconscious hip-hop music. For without the African ancestors and White abolitionists' fight for equality, we would not enjoy the privileges of recording music, enhancing better race relations, voting, reading, having a family, obtaining an education, exploring opportunities for achieving wealth legally, and the list goes on.

Despite those advances, some of hip-hop acts as the antithesis of everything our African ancestors fought for. Stereotypes about Blacks abound in the genre (i.e. ignorant, ostentatious, irresponsible, drug users, misogynistic, ghetto dwellers, sex driven, and so on). Hip-hop acts portray this monolithic image of the Black experience just to make a quick buck, forgetting the lessons we should have learned from our ancestors. It seems like the only time we want to exhibit that we have some semblance of ancestral home training is when we "get up at the MTV awards and *thank and praise my Lord and Savior Jesus Christ*"[3] for getting an award for the song: *Da Stupid Bitches in Da Hood Smokin' Crack.*[4] But hip-hop's beginnings did not start out this way. Before it became known as *hip-hop*, socially conscious *rap* music addressed the social injustices faced by Blacks and other ethnic minority groups[5]; a discussion on the difference between *rap* and *hip-hop* is forthcoming. Much of hip-hop music, on the other hand, has become so commercialized that it is no longer about social equality, but about a celebration of drugs, sex, guns, ghetto life, and money. These messages to Black and White youth propel them into their mis-education about

---

ii The reference to *our African ancestors* refers to all persons since I argue that all of us can trace our lineage and find African, Native, Irish, British, and a host of other ethnicities within it.

Black culture. It does not take a virtuoso of hip-hop to articulate this message—hip-hop videos oftentimes demonstrate it at every turn. A lifestyle of sex, drugs, big money, and crime is inculcated in the minds of many youth who grew up listening to hip-hop but not necessarily to those who grew up listening only to rap.

I'm Just Keepin' It Real: Celebrities and Hip-Hop Music

There seems to be a growing and prescient concern about hip-hop culture. Don Imus drew the ire of some in the hip-hop industry when he suggested that his reference to the Rutgers Women as *nappy headed hos* is no worse than how hip-hop artists treat Black women. Michael Richards, aka "Kramer" of *Seinfeld* fame, went into a tirade using the *n-word* as a means of attacking a comedy club's Black hecklers. Their comments drew more attention to the sad state of affairs of hip-hop artists who degrade African Americans. The April 16, 2007 episode of *The Oprah Winfrey Show* served as a catalyst to a discussion about the ways in which hip-hop is shaping the world's perceptions of Blacks. The women from Spelman College—a private, independent, liberal arts, historically Black college for women, founded in 1881—who were guest panelists on the show, charged that they are tired of the misogynist images in hip-hop. Nelly, a hip-hop artist, has been under fire by the women at Spelman College for his *Tip Drill* lyrics and video where he swiped a credit card down the derriere of a Black woman. Even Oprah's guest panelist, Stanley Crouch, stated that hip-hop may have become a minstrel show.

"Hip-hop's recent love affair with dance friendly tunes, light-hearted lyrics and questionable imagery have many wondering—have we become a minstrel show?" asks Demetria Lucas from *The Source,* a hip-hop magazine. She raises a good point as some hip-hop tunes and video have beats and images that originate from minstrel shows.

It may be for this reason that Nas, a rap artist, suggests that the hip-hop industry should be destroyed. Lucas and Nas' viewpoints to the community-at-large represent the need for a book that addresses how much of hip-hop music has become minstrelsy in nature and what we need to do to bring hip-hop back to meeting the tenets of rap.

Unconscious hip-hop has become markedly minstrelsy in nature. Minstrel shows—performed heavily during the 19th century by Whites in blackface—consisted of comedic skits, music, and dancing that portrayed the Black person as ignorant, misogynistic, lazy, greedy, and buffoonish. The minstrel show entertained Whites who watched actors in blackface portray stereotypic notions of Black culture. The actors earned hefty bucks for their interpretations of *keepin' it real* on what's going on among enslaved Black folks. Many Black male hip-hop artists follow the same prescriptive misogynistic, misanthropic formula that keeps White suburbanite youth begging for more since they are the largest buyers of hip-hop music. It gives meaning to the adage "The more things change, the more they remain the same." There appears to be few differences between the stereotypic Black man and woman portrayals during the minstrel show's heyday and the consequential abstractions of the bitches, niggas, hos, lazy, juvenile, and ignorant-acting persons portrayed in hip-hop music today. Songs peppered with such formulations should remind us of the old proverb: Those who do not learn from history are doomed to repeat it.

The derogatory language used by Imus and *Kramer* used mirrors the language used in much of hip-hop in the past 15 years. Does it take a White person—by however means necessary—to bring heavy media attention to what Black hip-hop male artists are saying about Black women to get people to become incendiary about it? The universe is inside every woman that ever lived, is living, or will live. And all hip-hop can say about the great contributions of the mothers that preceded them, that live among them, and will come after them is *Ay Bitch! Wait til you see my dick. Imma beat dat pussy up.*[6] Too many African queens have been dethroned, and the Black bitch is becoming nomenclature for Black women that come after her.

The chorus of Blacks who called for the immediate dismissal of Imus should ask what is the difference between a White male who earns a good living from degrading Black women and calls it *shock radio* and a Black male who earns a good living from degrading Black women and calls it *hip-hop*? Does Black America have a patent on taking liberties to demonstrate hatred towards itself while getting vehemently pissed off when White America take the same liberties? For instance, the term *nigga* is used among Blacks within Black communities. If White persons used the same term, many Blacks would scream, holler, protest, whine, cry, picket, sue, and demand an apology.

This complacency is a blatant backpedaling against the Civil Rights Movement where Blacks, Whites, Jews, and gays fought for equality and social justice. Rosa Parks, Bayard Rustin, Paul Robeson—and other seminal figures in the fight for Black equality— were not *niggas* and *bitches,* and for hip-hop music to embrace this term shows how much we have yet to learn about our true selves in Black history. For the very people rap music once sought to heal have now become in part a hip-hop target, and therefore, a source of the hurt African-Americans are experiencing today. Further, "major record labels, owned and controlled by Whites—the same labels that once ignored hip-hop completely—now control the direction of hip-hop. Record companies have learned what the

White masses want to hear—stories of Blacks killing Blacks, or occasionally Latinos killing Latinos; gangster artists who rap about ghetto violence are being signed by the thousands, with no regard for the effects on Black youth while the biggest consumers of it are suburban Whites."[7]

It is clearly an injustice, and an injustice anywhere is an injustice everywhere.[8] Civil Rights Activist Al Sharpton argues that some of the hip-hop artists who denigrate Blacks, and the patriarchal corporations that pay them, may take the stance that Civil Rights are something that occurred *back in the day*. For you are still 'back in the day' any time Black hip-hop artists are still referring to Blacks as niggers, and Black women as hos, bitches, and tricks. You are still in the day.[9] It will take all of us to make Martin Luther King Jr.'s dream come true in continuing to promote race relations positively within North America.

Barak Obama's election to the presidency marks a significant stride in the history of race relations. And Obama had the backing of some hip-hop artists who made songs relevant to him. It was during this period that elements of rap manifested itself in hip-hop. But the preponderance of mainstream hip-hop artists—even at this time of this writing—do not understand that a problem only exists if there is a difference between what is actually happening in the ghetto (hood) and what the artists' desire to be happening in the ghetto (hood).[10] How do the artists' stories about the *hood* translate into what the artist desires to happening in the *hood*?

The Argument's Focus

The 1712 Willie Lynch Letter serves as the theoretical basis of this text. It has been purported that Willie Lynch was slave owner who endeavored to educate White slave owners on how to maintain slavery of Blacks even after legalized slavery is *over*. Below is a portion of the letter that serves as the theoretical focus of this text:

> In my bag I have a full proof method of controlling Black slaves. I guarantee every one of you, if installed correctly, it will control the slaves for at least three hundred years. My method is simple, any member of your family or your overseer can use it. I have outlined a number of differences and I make them bigger. I use fear, distrust and envy for control purposes. These methods have worked on my modest plantation in the West Indies and they will work throughout the South. Take this simple list and think about it. On the top of my list is age, but it's only there because it starts with an A. The second is color or shade. There's intelligence, sex, size of plantation, status on plantation, attitude of owners, whether the slaves live in the valley or on a hill, north, east, south, or west, have fine hair or coarse hair, or is tall or short. Now that you have a list of differences I shall give you an outline of action. But before that, I shall assure you that distrust is stronger than trust, and envy is stronger than adulation, respect, or admiration. The Black slave, after receiving this indoctrination shall carry it on, and will become self-refueling and self generating for hundreds of years, maybe thousands of years. Now don't forget, you must pitch the old Black male against the young Black male, and the young Black male against the old Black male. You must use the female against the male, and you must use the male against the female. You must use the dark skinned slave against the light skinned slave, and the light skinned slave against the dark skinned slave. You

must also have your White servants and overseers distrust all Blacks, but it is necessary that your slaves trust and depend on us. They must love, respect and trust only us. Gentlemen, these keys are your keys to control. Use them, never miss an opportunity, and if used intensely for one year the slaves themselves will remain perpetually distrustful. Thank you, gentlemen.[11]

The Purpose of this Text

The Willie Lynch letter, which appeared on the Internet during the 1990s, contains obvious anachronisms considering some words did not come to be until well after 1712. In fact, some people argue that the term *lynching* comes from an eponymous descendent of Willie Lynch, while others argue that the letter is just an Internet hoax designed to disrupt the healing process that ethnic minorities are still undergoing due to the effects of slavery and racism. Whatever the case, this work does not endeavor to prove or disapprove the authenticity of the Willie Lynch letter, nor to provide any background information relative to Lynch's actual or imagined existence. This work only endeavors to examine motifs that pervade most of hip-hop in connection with the information contained in the so-named Willie Lynch letter, whether or not the letter is historically accurate. The intent is NOT to degrade any hip-hop artist, group, or affiliates. This work does not seek to air out Black and White folks' dirty laundry, largely because it makes no sense to air out a dirty garment without first getting to the root of how to clean the dirt. We have to confront the dirt of complacency where Blacks call other Blacks and their children *nigga*, *bitch*, *ho* and *trick* while our White youth are helping to throw the dirt not realizing the impact it has on their viewpoints of Blackness. I am glad that

New York City made a resolution to ban the usage of *nigger*; I am glad that the NAACP had a funeral service burying *nigger* and its descendants: cousin *nigga,* uncle *niggrah,* and aunt *negress.* But these collective actions have only killed the body not the soul. This legacy of *nigger, bitch, ho,* and *trick* has to die a slow death, and we will have to train all of the youth that come after us how to dismantle its hold and destroy it once and for all. So when they air out the laundry, it won't be soiled with self-hatred but freshened with self-love.

So the purpose of *The 21ˢᵗ Century Hip-Hop Minstrel Show: Are We Continuing in the Blackface Tradition?* is fourfold: 1) to initiate dialogue on how minstrelsy and oppression have become dominant motifs within much of mainstream hip-hop music; 2) to present how the elements within the Willie Lynch Letter are used within hip-hop music as a method of keeping Blacks psychologically enslaved; 3) to argue that hip-hop music appears on the surface to enhance Black and White race relations when in actuality, White youth via Black hip-hop music are adopting hip-hop verbiage and clothing styles without knowing the historical significance behind what they say and what they wear. Thus, once these White youth become adults, they have stereotypic knowledge of Black people that they will inevitably pass to their children. If then they are accused of being racist or sexist for repeating what hip-hop has taught them, they are oblivious as to the source of their acts of racism or sexism. White children acquire racism as a matter of course through observing and internalizing the values within their environment and act accordingly. Many of the misogynistic and Black self-hatred themes within hip-hop confirm what some Whites might have been taught about Blacks; and not by their own volition, they perpetuate the cycle of racism and sexism. And the last purpose of this text is 4) to offer what Black and White lovers of hip-hop can do collectively to start dismantling the remnants of slavery to contribute to the racial healing process. For starters, Bankole poses:

> How can African people talk about [social justice, equal opportunity, and race relations] or attempt to effectively operationalize these concepts when there is the instance of (though often understated) self-hatred? Another question is, how are we to unify and progressively address the major problems in the Black community, which are consuming the masses of our people, if we cannot (once and for all), consolidate the fact of who we are? Is it any wonder then, that some of our people, believe ... that the word 'nigger' actually can and should be used as a term of endearment among Black people? This includes the overarching pimp/prostitute theme in U.S. popular culture: the terms 'bitch' and 'ho' to refer to Black womanhood; and 'gangsta', 'G', 'mack', 'player', and 'dog' to refer to Black manhood.[12]

Such themes have become a part of the cavalcade of Black masculinity. In accomplishing this purpose of discussing how some themes in hip-hop music curry favor with motifs of slavery, this text addresses the following components of the Willie Lynch letter: age, intelligence, east versus west, status on plantation, Black males versus Black females, and slaves who trust and depend on *us*.

Disclaimers

Hip-hop music has the potential to empower youth to make a positive difference. All hip-hop is not negative. There are several hip-hop artists who are giving back to the community. The intent of this text is not to take a negative slant to hip-hop music. It does seek to initiate honest dialogue on how niggas, bitches, hos, and tricks are consequential identities of hip-hop, and why there is a negative slant on what is being portrayed in hip-hop. This text does not advocate for the censorship of hip-hop music; every person has a constitutional right to free speech. Neither is this text an attack on Blacks, Whites, women, men, teens, or youth. Black is beautiful; but so is White, Asian, Mexican, Latino, and any other race. We have failed Martin Luther King Jr.'s dream if we do not recognize that brothers and sisters come in different colors. This text is meant to challenge all readers to consider assessing how *unconscious* hip-hop music negatively affects the healing of race relations in North America and how it exacerbates racial hatred in other parts of the world. Further, those of us who are socially conscious cannot make the mistake of trying to coerce social consciousness upon others we consider naïve. Today, we cannot look to comedians, hip-hop artists, or ball players for political direction since their *role* is to entertain. However, this book endeavors to begin a dialogue that may act as a springboard to get entertainers, leaders, school teachers, preachers, *thugs, gangstas, wankstas,* the general public, and you meaningfully engaged in analyzing the images shown via hip-hop. And it asks the community to wield their resources to serve the masses. The job is not hip-hop artists alone; it is yours and mine. Black people may be a rock's throw from destroying everything our White and Black ancestors have taught us. It takes a village to raise a child. We must become the village that raises our youth as representatives of the royal lineage to which they are successors. This book, *The 21ˢᵗ Century Hip-Hop Minstrel Show: Are We Continuing the Blackface Tradition?* is just part of my contribution to this effort.

Chapter One

CHAPTER ONE: HIP-HOP'S ADULTEROUS
AFFAIRS WITH THE MINSTREL SHOW

History repeats itself: first as a tragedy and then as a farce.[13]

—*Karl Marx*

Use your brain! It's not them that's killing us; it's us that's killing us.[14]

—*Tupac*

In the Willie Lynch Letter, which made its grand debut on the Internet in the 1990s, Lynch describes how to keep Blacks enslaved long after slavery has officially ended. We know little about Lynch; we do not even know if he ever existed. We do not know if the Letter is authentic. However, the infamous Letter should give White and Black America pause to consider exactly how applicable the Letter is to the musical aspects of American society, more specifically mainstream hip-hop. Some corporate recording companies, the *real* driving force behind unconscious hip-hop music, are following the Letter's blueprint to keeping

Black youth psychologically enslaved while mis-educating White youth.

Unconscious hip-hop is the most influential force that governs youths' behavior, style, mannerisms, attitudes, ideologies, and dress around the world. What youth see in the hip-hop videos is what they are subject to becoming and/or imitating. *Unconscious hip-hop music* synthesizes false attitudes and thoughts about Blacks into a visual pattern reflective of corporate America's power to perpetuate Black stereotypes and skew reality. The sprinkling of linguistic gems such as *bitch, ho, pimp,* and *nigga* within hip-hop music give delineations of Black culture worse than the racist slur Sambo, more offensive than Jim Crow, and far more destructive than Uncle Ben and Zip Coon. The source of these themes is the minstrel show.

Minstrel Shows in Its Heyday

While the Willie Lynch Letter was *allegedly* delivered in 1712, the minstrel show made its debut in the late 1700s. The English actor who donned blackface would perform the role of Negro to White audiences. The actor would make a parody of the Negro using patter, dance, humor, and song to convey the Negro's dialect, inability to read, treatment of women, childishness, and attempts to educate self and fit in with Whites. By the 19th century, the minstrel theater had become incredibly popular in America; minstrel shows represented the national consciousness of America.

The popularity of minstrel shows is attributable to Thomas Rice, Bill Whitlock, Dick Pelham, and Dan Emmett who were among the first group of minstrels. Thomas Rice's *Jim Crow* had a song and dance—and era during segregation—that kept White audiences in derision at the expense of Blacks. Later, Whites wished to have a more authentic representation of Blacks by having Black actors wear blackface and perpetuate exaggerated stereotypes of Blacks. Instantly, the minstrel show, making mockery of the cultural and stereotypical aspects of Negros, "transformed regional differences of language into signs of racial inferiority."[15] These shows caused White audiences to erupt in even greater gales of giggles. And today, they are giggling all the way to the bank as they make money off the hip-hop artist who is pitching age-old messages of ignorance, hate, crime, and juvenile behavior all in the name of representing the ghetto (hood).

Jibbs, a teenage hip-hop artist, had a smash hit in 2006 entitled *Chain Hang Low*. Jibbs asserts that he got the beat to his single from "… the ice cream truck. The Mister Softee truck was always riding around my block in St. Louis and the kids sang it everyday."[16] In fact, the beat was borrowed from a minstrel show entitled *Zip Coon* with a song and character of the same name. Zip Coon was a one-dimensional Black minstrel character who mimicked Whites' speech and dress. He often donned flashy jewels and chased women for the purpose of adding to his female repertoire. Stepin Fetchit, a stage name for Black comedian and actor Lincoln Theodore Perry, further popularized this image in the 1920s. The song *Zip Coon* morphed into the song *Do Your Ears Hang Low*. The 1928 cartoon *Steamboat Willie,* where Mickey Mouse made his debut, also featured the tune.

Perry's success was largely due to Whites swallowing his act as the accurate representation of Black people. Hip-hop has sold this representation to White and Black hip-hop youth. When White youth adopt Black hip-hop styles, they can easily disown them without stigmatization. To add, Melvin Donaldson told Bakari Kitwana, author of *Why White Kids Love Hip-Hop* (2005):

With blackface you can take it off. White hip-hop kids can turn their caps around, put a belt in their pants and go to the mall without being followed. Black people have to deal with oppression, but also character types that the hip-hop industry has created with the music by continuing the thug and gangsta stereotypes about Blacks. White hip-hop kids can pick and choose without repercussions and the full weight of stereotypes.

White students at Tarleton State University in Texas celebrated the Martin Luther King Jr. holiday by hosting a campus party inviting Black stereotypes to serve the liquor, play the music, and provide visual entertainment. The kids dressed as Aunt Jemina, wore dreadlocked wigs, donned bandanas and baggy clothing to give an image of *gang* and *hood* life, and took pictures in various poses honoring the malt liquor. The kids charged that the party was not meant to be racist; rather, they wanted to get to know the realities of other Black kids.[17]

In a similar fashion, law students from the University of Connecticut held a *Bullets and Bubbly* party where the future lawyers donned baggy clothing and held guns. In a similar fashion, the University of Colorado's Ski and Snowboard club advertised a gangsta party. The theme was fostered on fliers with pictures of hip-hop artists bearing fake bullet holes. Not to be outdone, Clemson University held a party with a similar theme where a White student added cushion in her pants to make her derriere appear wider while another student wore blackface. When hip-hop music presents such images, no fuss is made about it. However, when White college kids imitate such images, Blacks see it as a problem. It is a problem regardless of what race is placed on it.

Brief History of Rap

Rap music was born at 1520 Sedgwick Avenue, South Bronx, NY in the 1970s.[18] Rap started with deejays replacing disco music. Afrika Bambaataa, Grandmaster Flash, and Kool Herc were just some of the pioneers. Bambaataa music incorporated elements of the civil rights movement with Malcolm and Martin's speeches overshadowing the instrumentals (much like the songs hip-hop artists recorded in honor of their support for Barak Obama). Grandmaster Flash was an expert in mixing and remixing beats; he is credited with inventing the sampling machine. Kool Herc threw block parties that centered on consciousness raising and having a good time. Chic's "Good Times" and Sugar Hill Gang's "Rappers Delight" were among the first major rap hits.

Five elements of rap music are: deejaying, graffiti, b-boying/b-girling, emceeing, and having knowledge, culture, and overstanding.

Deejaying

A disc jockey is better known as a DJ. This person may play albums or compact discs at clubs, parties, radio, or concerts. Deejaying is one foundational element of rap. Clive Campbell, aka Kool Herc, was deejaying at his party in 1971 at the Sedgwick Avenue Community Center. This community was known for gang violence and sociopolitical and socioeconomic decline. This party was about bringing peace within the community through rap music. The music healed gang relations; Herc got the gangs to focus on what they were hearing. He mixed the break sections of a few selected records together in sequence without playing the beginning or ending of each corresponding song, fading one song directly into the next.[19]

Graffiti

Youth in the inner-city during the 1970s and 80s used graffiti on various kinds of property to express their concerns, wants, and needs for their communities. These youth believed graffiti was one way to communicate with to adults who otherwise would not listen to them. Youth used walls, trains, subways, bridges, almost anything stationary to spell out their messages and to show adults their intelligence and talent.

B-boying/B-girling

Dancing was a major part of rap culture. Self-taught dancers would incorporate floorspins, acrobatic gestures, and fancy footwork as part of their repertoire. The urbandictionary.com suggests that the 'B' in b-boying/b-girling stands for break. The break had no vocals, just instrumentation. The boys and girls break danced while the instrumentation was played. The double-dutch and the electric boogie are examples.

MCing

The MC's responsibility during the early days of rap was to assist the DJ and to keep the crowd engaged in the music. In doing so, they might tell a story or command the crowd to chant phrases. Some notable MCs, or master of ceremonies, are Kurtis Blow, Kool Moe Dee, and Queen Latifah.

Knowledge, Culture, and Overstanding

Afrika Bambaataa and the Universal Zulu Nation charge that collectively knowledge, culture, and overstanding is the fifth element of rap music. Bambaataa advocated for rap to hold fast to the collective consciousness that was its foundation to the culture. Rap music articulated knowledge to its listeners about the struggles members of the culture were experiencing. As rap evolved into hip-hop, financial gain became more paramount than knowledge, culture, and activism. Bambaataa did not wish to see this evolution. He coined the term *overstanding* which has roots in the Rastafarian ideology of nonconformity.

Where is the presence of all five of these elements in hip-hop music? If they are not present, then how can *hip-hop* and *rap* be used interchangeably? Socially conscious rap has become vestigial while mainstream hip-hop reigns ubiquitously.

Rap's Evolution into Hip-Hop

Rap music's beginnings held an international influence. DJ Kool Herc was born in Jamaica (as well as Sandra "Pepa" Denton of Salt-N-Pepa). Doug E. Fresh, known as the human beatbox, was born in Barbados; Richard Walters, better known as "Slick Rick" is from London, England. Afrika Bambaataa and DJ Grandmaster Flash, while born in the United States, have cultural roots in Barbados. Rap music was not born in Jamaica, Barbados, or London; but in Bronx, New York out of circumstances of poverty and marginalization in the United States. These groundbreaking artists provided the foundation of making rap, and later hip-hop, international.

During the second wave of rap came Run DMC, LL Cool J, Kool Moe Dee, Big Daddy Kane, Fat Boys, UTFO, and Roxanne Shante. Run DMC's "Walk the Way" with Aerosmith launched rap's crossover into the White market. Music by these artists was characterized by partying, machoism, and dissing.

Following this wave came political or message rap by artists such as Public Enemy, The Last Poets, Queen Latifah, and MC Hammer. The prevalent themes in their music were African culture, self-respecting, and societal ills against ethnic minorities.

Around the early 1990s, gangsta rap emerged. Gangsta rap was a product of gang culture and street wards of South Central, Compton, and Long Beach. The music's message was delivered by NWA (*Niggaz Wit Attitude*), Geto Boys, and Ice-T. This music was characterized by forty-ounce malt liquor, killing, hypermasculinity, and blunts.

From gangsta rap, booty rap emerged. The group, Two Live Crew was a forerunner. Duice's "Daisy Dukes" and Tag Team's "Whoop There It Is" set the thematic tone for songs of this genre to be characterized by an obsession with sex and eroticism, visually backed by scantily clothed women, heavy base beats, *niggas*, and *beeyatches*. Luke's song "Asshole Naked" guarantees that he serves as the narrator of the salacious action viewers see in his videos. Hip-hop artists at this point moved on a pendulum swing from using elements of rap's early beginnings to moving increasingly to criminal and sexual themes. Later, Ludacris, Nelly, Snoop Dogg, and 50 Cent got into the act, seemingly competing to compete for which videos would contain the most bodies that some wet dreams are made of.

Difference Between *Rap* and *Hip-Hop*

The civil rights movement provided Black and White America with a voice that spoke eloquently to the masses. We had Martin, Malcolm, Mary, Maxine, Rosa, Fannie, C. Dolores, Thurgood, Jesse, Frank, Andrew, Michael, Al and countless Jews and Whites who spoke on social injustices at the risk of being jailed, threatened, persecuted, and/or killed.[20] The privileges Blacks have today are thanks in part to these civil rights pioneers, and these privileges we have today were not provided voluntarily. Our ancestors and pioneers encountered resistance that caused them to be spied on, lied to, criticized, and killed. After the civil rights movement ended in the late 1960s, social injustices in the Black community were not completely assuaged since injustice was still rampant in many of the communities.

Rap music's initial purpose was to be a platform to entertain and educate the United States on the social and political realities that still plagued the lives of Blacks and Latinos.[21] Some of their realities included discrimination, poverty, police brutality, and racial profiling. Some of **rap** music's earliest artists were Afrika Bambaataa, (who is the founder of Zulu Nation, an organization built upon principles of love, peace, and unity), Grand Master Flash, Sugarhill Gang, Kurtis Blow, The Sequence, Whodini, UTFO, and the Fat Boys. Chuck D from Public Enemy asserts that rap—which is socially conscious—is "about attacking the status quo"[22] whereas hip-hop—much of it is socially unconscious—is a marketable entity where some record corporations exploit what they believe are stereotypical aspects of Black culture; they profit from it at astronomical heights at the expense of the Black hip-hop artist. Rap music in its infancy addressed Black pride, poverty, dancing, and social injustice, and thus "is a form of oppositional culture that offers a message of resistance, empowerment, and social critique."[23] This message is a part of preserving the cultural past of West African slaves who used oral traditions and set them to music.

However, Black Entertainment Television (BET) does not show multi-dimensional videos about the Black experience nor does it provide its youthful viewers with varied hip-hop musical choices.

The main reason lies in that it is camouflaged via BET's *106 N Park*'s Top 10 countdown where viewers have to call in for the best songs and pay a fee. A former BET producer contends that BET is aiding and abetting in the destruction of hip-hop. This producer notes that the call-in aspect of the show is a waste of time since BET determines what order the videos will be played and ranked. He adds that almost every hip-hop artist is a caricature of the thug image.[24]

For example, Tupac was the first rapper to use the term *thug life* in his lyrics which was his acronym for: *The hate u gave little infants fucks everybody.* But this meaning was redefined after record corporations saw this image as a cash cow. Tupac was a socially conscious rapper who was not taken seriously until his work became less about social consciousness and more about corporate gain. Tupac was captured on camera spitting, modeling bling, bling, displaying money, and disrespecting women. But youth adopted what they believed was Tupac's style and persona at this point. It was part of the record exploitation process. Even Afeni Shakur, Tupac's mother, stated: "You are not going to be in the hip-hop industry and not be exploited."[25]

I Know You Not Gonna Play THAT Song: Civil Rights and Hip-hop

C. Delores Tucker, a civil rights political activist, vocalized in the early 1990s that obscenities in hip-hop are subtle forms of genocide for African-Americans. In the wake of the Imus slur, William Tucker, husband of the late activist, noted that Imus' comment "brought about a revival of the struggle she waged, literally, by herself for the past fourteen years."[26] More Blacks are beginning to re-evaluate the civil rights leader's prophetic message. But the civil rights pioneers cannot celebrate that Blacks have overcome if the hip-hop generation has no idea how to build on the rights now afforded to them. To many youth, John Hope Franklin, Maxine Waters, Maya Angelou, and Dorothy Height combined are less regarded than Lil Wayne, Ying Yang Twins, Lil John, Flava Flav, and Lil' Kim. People of African descent should engage in a blitzkrieg effort to help Black and White youth take advantage of our accessible collective histories, which will aid them in a critical analysis of hip-hop lyrics that contradict those histories.

No longer focusing on matters of poverty, police brutality, and infiltration of drugs within inner-city communities—a baton that was passed to hip-hop—rap emerged into hip-hop in the early 1990s. It was during this time that rap was incapacitated by the power of financial greed—an avarice that diminished its political heft and apparently left its capacity for empowering the masses quite scathed. The themes of "pimp, pimping, pimp juice, pimp paraphernalia like goblets and canes, the pimp lifestyle, ethos and 'code of honor' have permeated hip-hop culture and beyond."[27] From this pimp ideology, television viewers can choose from a number of pimp-themed flicks to tickle their fancies: *Pimp My Ride* hosted by Xzibit, *Lil Pimp* with Ludacris and Lil' Kim about a nine-year-old White suburbanite boy who takes up pimping, and *Muthafuckin' P.I.M.P.* as 50 Cent calls himself in his video. And there is Nelly's *Pimp Juice* that may quench the appetites of viewers who salivate like Pavlov's dog during the showing of any soft-porn hip-hop video. If that is not enough, there is Bishop's *Pimplicious* voice tone and screen saver and Three Six Mafia's "It's Hard out Here for a Pimp." And to finish this multi-course meal, one can relax in an NPA—National Pimping Association—T-shirt. We cannot help but ask ourselves after listening to the motherlode of these less-than-ear-delicious themes: Did Martin Luther King Jr.

die a martyr so we can spread the message to White America via its record companies about pimping when the reality is that Black mainstream hip-hop artists are being pimped? These artists are convinced of their genius and ability to degrade self while degrading Black history and the Black race. And many young Black girls and Black women endure a ceaseless barrage of acrimony from them, ignoring how the hip-hop artists' tabloidesque persona and marketable story—true or no—are what makes the record company—not the artist—a boatload of dough. Sadly, the money made hardly ever gets used to build up the downtrodden communities often referenced to in hip-hop.

Chuck D adds that many hip-hop artists have to foster the stereotypical aspects since they believe it is the sole way to "become megastars" in "presenting themselves in a negative light." Further, "African American record executives, from Russell Simmons to P. Diddy to Suge Knight, have unashamedly had as significant a hand in peddling stereotypical images of Black Americans as their white counterparts, even as the major labels hold the most influential cards. ... So whether, say, Dr. Dre is in Ruthless Records, Death Row or Aftermath clothing doesn't sway the final outcome. He's still advancing images of Blacks that reinforce stereotypes at the same time as they reveal an emerging new Black youth culture."[28] For example, Tupac's earlier rap albums dealt with issues of pro-Blackness, social injustice, and poverty. It appeared that the masses were not paying attention to what he had to say. Hence, he shifted to a 'bad boy' image, which garnered him *hip-hop* celebratory status, and the more he exuded this 'bad boy' image, the greater his fame. Tupac's new image is the antithesis of his background since he was strongly influenced by the civil rights movement, Martin Luther King, Malcolm X and the Black Panthers.[29]

Many rap artists in the early to mid-1980s had middle-class backgrounds; Kitwana (2005) adds that

> some even were college educated. This shifted dramatically by the 1990s, when many of the big-name rap stars to emerge had origins in poor and working-class communities. This fact helped give voice to the early 1990s expression 'keep it real.' Although the trend of rising incarceration began in the mid- to- late 1970s, it isn't until the late 1980s that we began to see the lines blur between prison culture and hip-hop culture, given the numbers of young Black men entering and exiting the criminal justice system. So the shifting content of hip-hop lyrics from the mid-1980s era, when the content seemed more diverse, to the 1990s street culture—dominated lyrics and so-called gangsta style was not strictly coincidental. Additionally, the terms 'nigga' and 'bitch' in reference to young Black men and women in hip-hop didn't gain significant frequency until the early 1990s. This has more to do with prison culture than with class. ...[30]

Growing up in the 70s and 80s, it was not in my realm of consciousness to deem any person a *nigga* or *bitch*. During that time, *dems fightin' words*.

Hip-hop artist Ja Rule describes hip-hop as being commercial. He adds that "There is so much money in it now. Big companies like Nike and Pepsi see an opportunity to make money ... so it's just not as pure as it was." He argues that hip-hop is about "niggas and beeyatches, power and money."[31] It is the antithesis of rap's foundation. Hip-hop exchanged social consciousness for guns, gangs, violence, drugs, and niggas to capture the interest of suburbanites.

Hip-hop has become a capitalist mercenary designed to misrepresent Black culture and is being paid by corporations to do so. All of the five elements of rap are not present in hip-hop music, for they served as the instrumentalities that work in unison to generate the change that empowered Blacks en masse.

Darius Pridgen, pastor of *True Bethel Baptist Church*, suggests that hip-hop is not akin to civil rights. From his perspective, hip-hop has become a vehicle by which youth act out what they see in videos while those persons who engineer hip-hop are watching more jails being built for those youth. These same persons are financing the hip-hop artists so that they may have big pools, houses, and jewelry, but in return the hip-hop artist must engage Black youth in self-genocide in the name of being angry—even though they may not know what they should be angry about—but masquerading as self-expression.[iii]

A noted feminist critic, bell hooks, adds that much of hip-hop is "expressive of the cultural crossings, mixings, and engagement of black youth culture with the values, attitudes, and concerns of the white majority."[32] Luke, of 2 Live Crew fame, charges that part of what the White *male* majority wanted was to see more Black women with "big asses" in videos. For better or worse, sex is the driving force behind hip-hop.[33] Peter Loewenberg is convinced that "when forbidden desires emerge in a white man, he can facilitate their repression by projecting them onto blacks or members of other racial minorities. In the unconscious of the bigot the black represents his own repressed instincts which he fears and hates and which are forbidden by his conscience as it struggles to conform to the values professed by society. This is why the black man becomes

---

iii This interview was conducted with Pastor Darius Pridgen True Bethel Baptist Church, Buffalo, New York.

the personification of sexuality, lewdness, laziness, dirtiness, and unbridled hostility."[34]

Thus, while Blacks have created hip-hop culture, corporate America takes it and sells it back to Blacks and tells them: 'This is what Blackness is."[35] Hip-hop may have turned "into a field where only those who have been shot, committed crimes and spent time in jail are ... worthy of studio recordings."[36] Mainstream hip-hop artists' feigned ignorance seems to know no boundaries. This statement carries the notion that hip-hop music has been reduced to synchronizing prison and music where "corporate [hip-hop] soundtracks promote lifestyles that are actually 'deathstyles' ... and this helps foster the perception of lawlessness that leads to the criminalization of our Hip-hop generation."[37] It is part of the exploitation process.

But behind this criminalization are record companies. The modus operandi of some White-owned recording companies is to take control of the genres of music Blacks have created and profit from them. Elvis, who is still feted as one of the greatest singers who ever lived, reworked Black songs that became hits. Rock, blues, jazz, and hip-hop were an integral part of Black cultural entertainment but have become so commercialized that the true characteristics of the genres are unrecognizable.

In the process, many hip-hop artists may be achieving wealth but not using their influence to wield political power for all Black people. They are consistently braggadocio about how much they have versus how much other Blacks do not have (particularly in the form of houses, cars, money, and women; but yet the media sharing the news about the high number of foreclosures among the artists). Wise Intelligent challenges us to

Imagine for a minute if Harriet Tubman would have adopted this same selfish position, and after she 'made-it' to freedom, or after 'achieving' that freedom and realizing her 'dream' of being a free-woman, said 'I can't save the world' and went shopping in Paris? Well, she didn't and she knew that she could not 'save the world' but believed deeply that she could 'save the BLACK WORLD' so she ACTIVELY got involved and organized the 'Underground Railroad!' She is the 'Poster-Child' for a 'sister' who 'made-it' to freedom, became the 'realization of a dream' but understood that the 'dream' was not fulfilled unless it was shared by the 'masses.' Proper Education Always Counters Exploitation. ...[38]

The popularity of hip-hop music is fueled by some of corporate America's desire to validate their preconceptions about most Black males. Mos Def argues that the derogatory lyrics and images in hip-hop are entertainment to Whites; "we're adopting their morals like we them and we never been them. We don't have the same struggle. Dudes is no more than 20 years removed from real poverty. For dudes to have this much access to money and it's not translating to people power, it's inexcusable."[39]

When rap's themes advocated for justice and equality it was labeled as racist, tension-building, and destructive music. Groups like *A Tribe Called Quest*, *Public Enemy*, and *KRS-One*[40] have experienced harsh criticism because of the content of their progressive music. However when hip-hop promotes the gangster, pimp, nigga, or ho of the week, it does not create any havoc.[41]

Who is doing the promoting? Record companies have been influential in reshaping conscious rap—that told truths about the injustices Blacks and Latinos were faced with—into hip-hop that is becoming more gimmicky in theme. Hip-hop has leaked a satchel of scenarios about *how much money I got, how many bitches I'm sexing, how much bling, bling I got, how I come from the 'hood* and other themes of buffoonery. Hip-hop is serving as the surrogate father for many Black male youth. This prodigal parent is teaching falsities about masculinity, women, education, voting, Black history, and sex education.

Simply chronicling the wreckage, these socially unconscious hip-hop artists strive for what they perceive as surrogate patriarchy by 1) hosting lighter-skinned females with bone straight hair in their videos; 2) treating women as second-class citizens; 3) serving as an oppressor of the Black race; 4) commercializing hip-hop only to increase hefty corporate America's pockets while mis-educating and misleading youth; and 5) rescinding any responsibility for any youth who mimic their studio *gangsta* behavior; that is, to blame parents, community, and everyone else for the actions of youth listening to the music. The media take pains to insulate hip-hop from any wrongdoing, but the strongest argument made by unconscious hip-hop artists is, 'The parents need to do a better job of monitoring what their kids are watching and hearing. If you don't like the music, turn it off.' If only if were that simple. Children and young adults aged 3–21 are accessing *soft porn* (ahem!) *hip-hop music* anytime and anywhere outside the home in this technologically-advanced society. Even if they could not access the music, they cannot help but be influenced by witnessing other kids engage in a day-in-and-day-out basis the clothing, language, tattooing, sexuality, fashion, mannerisms, and porn that have become the additional elements of hip-hop. The media has known for a long time that music establishes fashion and behavior trends; with this barometer, children decide what sayings and styles are *in* and what is *out*.

Corporate record companies are making big profits off of these false images of Blacks while commanding the Black hip-hop artist to continue such degradation of his people. It brings to mind how White men commanded Black men to beat Fannie Lou Hamer for attempting to register to vote. Mrs. Hamer remembered that one of the officers said to the Black inmates: "I want you to make that bitch wish she was dead." He also threatened the black inmates that if they didn't use the blackjack on her, "You know what I'll use on you." Mrs. Hamer asked the Black inmate: "You mean you would do this to your own race?"[42] The inmate commenced beating her until she passed out; I surmise that those injuries were what eventually killed her at a swifter pace than her diabetes and hypertension.

Whatever is not helping you is hurting you. Unconscious hip-hop with its injurious references to Black women as bitches or piece of ass have taught a generation of youth to see these women in such light. If this trend continues, it will eventually kill the Black woman. Black and White youth do not have any experience to counteract the images they see in hip-hop videos and thus they act out what they see and hear without question. They interfuse reality and fantasy because while some adults in the record industry are feeding youth globs of sex, other adults are not taking the time to teach youth that they are being targeted. Then the question is often asked: What is wrong with our kids today? What is wrong is that we are talking about our kids but not talking to them about their history and legacy as citizens of the universe.

Hip-hop artists are the first to enjoy the labor of Martin Luther King Jr. and the Civil Rights Movement. The Civil Rights Movement was a youth movement that changed discriminatory laws so that Blacks born during the 1970s had rights and privileges that were not immediately afforded to them. The ancestors that came before them provided the movement's blueprint. Those youth who were part of the movement knew their history; they knew the power of faith, prayer, civil disobedience, education, and perseverance. When the torch was passed to the rap artists in the 1970s, they created songs that were uplifting, that spoke about love, peace, unity, and equality. When the torch was passed to the hip-hop artists in the 1990s, it burned down to embers, a shadow of its former flame.

It seems only yesterday that our society was released from segregation, Jim Crow, Blackface, and racial oppression—and yet, while some of these societal ills have reared their ugly heads again, many hip-hop artists are being used as leaders to destroy everything our civil rights leaders did to provide all of us with rights never before enjoyed. A preacher changed the most powerful nation in the world. Martin Luther King Jr. followed his philosophy: "After one has discovered what he [or she] is called for, he [or she] should set out to do it with all of the power that he [or she] has in his [or her] system. ... Do it as if God Almighty ordained you at this particular moment in history to do it."[43]

Thus, from my circumspective perception, I contend that rap spans from the late-1970s to the early 1990s; and hip-hop was born in the early 1990s. Some persons born after 1973 saw rap morph into hip-hop and were exposed as teens to visual and lyrical misogyny, degradation, and interracial oppression. During the 1990s, corporations saw potential profit for capitalizing on hip-hop more than they saw with rap music. They adopted this imperialist mindset in much of the same way the British Empire sought to take over Africa to profit from its wealth.[44] They began to have hip-hop music initially target teens in the early 1990s to convince them to endorse and embrace being niggas, bitches, hos, gang bangers, or a combination thereof. These same teens were slated to get on the path of acting out said roles vis-à-vis their disregard of Black history. At the time of this writing, these teens are now in their mid-thirties, and corporations have looked at the teens, twenty-somethings, and early-thirty-somethings as a massive domain to colonize using weapons of hip-hop films, music, clothing, and magazines. These corporations initially had nothing to do with hip-hop; but camouflaged their capitalist interest by using Black hip-hop artists to exploit other Blacks for major profit. Hip-hop artists now assume the marketing models used by corporations; corporate control of hip-hop is being used "to destroy African-Americans and particularly, African-American youth culturally, socially, and intellectually while reducing them to economic cattle ripe for exploitation."[45] This exploitation is guised as *keeping in real* while hip-hop artists are using degradation as a means to *credentialize* hip-hop and mistakenly calling it a socially empowering genre of music. Clearly rap music addressed great particularities about social injustice among Blacks while hip-hop presents gross generalities about stereotypical Blackness.

Youth Caught Under the Spell

The millennium generation of youth born between 1985 and 2004 was born into hip-hop. Much of this hip-hop audience is under hypnosis. And it is not their fault that they do not know about the importance of Afrika Bambaataa, Public Enemy, or Kurtis Blow. It is OUR fault, those of us who grew up listening to conscious rap music, learning about the continued struggles for equality. It is OUR fault, that our churches did not take the lead in commandeering efforts to empower our youth while the rest of the world was trying to convince our Black youth that they are bitches, niggas, and dogs. It is OUR fault, that we have an ADULT problem, not a youth problem. It is OUR fault that we have allowed OUR heritage to be systematically expunged by the aiding and abetting of unconscious hip-hop music. It is OUR fault that many of our youth are innocuously perpetuating the stereotypes we have been trying to overcome. It is OUR fault that many of our youth have embraced a culture that does not have a vision for uplifting the masses; but our youth are imitating them and are still directionless. We have to ask our youth to forgive us for falling short. But we can begin to work together to help us all do some *unlearning* about the very stereotypes we have adopted, fostered, believed, or practice about Blacks as perpetuated by hip-hop music.

Stereotypes of Blacks for Sale

Historically, stereotypes have been the vehicles that represent patriarchal perspectives on Blacks. Some of the common stereotypes of Blacks as presented in some hip-hop songs are: lazy, drug sellers, drug abusers, ignorant, irresponsible, full of baby-daddy or baby-momma drama, ghetto dwellers, criminals, destructive, sexually unrestrained, womanizing, niggers (or niggas), prone to Black-on-Black crime, among others. How many of these stereotypes are sold within hip-hop music? How often do we hear about Blacks protesting against these false images of Blackness? These stereotypes are being sold to youth around the world who imitate what they see; many youth do not realize that "whatever you do **most** will be what you do **best**!"[46] Hip-hop artists make a pretty penny exuding a misogynistic and criminalizing image. Hutchinson points out that in a confessional moment Snoop Dogg told interviewers that the lyrics of his gangsta rap did not depict his life or reality. Snoop says he does it for the money. Even Snoop realizes that MONEY + STEREOTYPE = MO' MONEY.[47]

But the major players who distribute, package, and sell these stereotypical images are Sony, Warner Brothers, EMI, MCA, BMG, and Polygram. Hip-hop critic Bakari Kitwana adds:

> Often highlighted are those aspects of [hip-hop] which … do not threaten the status quo, reinforce negative stereotypes about Blacks, [and] manipulate those stereotypes to increase sales. … Countless artists in search of securing record deals report that they are often told that their message is not hard enough, that they are too clean-cut, that 'hardcore' is what is selling now. …[48]

Record companies that produce this debasing merry-go-around are shafting mainstream hip-hop Black artists and their listeners all over the world with every gyration.

Blacks did raise quite a fuss about David Chang's board game *Ghettopoly*, charging that it promoted negative images about Blacks.[49] Some of the images of the Asian-American's board game include 40 ounces of malt liquor, drug selling, carjacking, guns, rocks (of crack), and an insensitive mocking of Dr. Martin Luther King Jr.'s *I Have a Dream*. Chang explained that watching MTV and playing video games taught him all he needed to know about Black America in order to create an authentic gaming experience any player would treasure. These stereotypes carry over in how mass media shapes our "image of the world and then tells us what to think about that image; essentially everything we know—or think we know—about events outside our own neighborhood or circle of acquaintances comes to us via our daily newspaper, our weekly news magazine, our radio, or our television. … For example, the way in which the news is covered: which items are emphasized and which are played down, the reporter's choice of words, tone of voice, and facial expressions; the wording of headlines; the choice of illustrations—all of these things subliminally and yet profoundly affect the way in which we interpret what we see or hear."[50]

Some of these hip-hop artists still insist they are just *tryna keep it real* while *reppin' their hood* in the videos. These same artists do not convey that they go to their upscale homes and drive tony cars; and they do not hang around the ghetto—whether they are from it or not. Studio hip-hop artists are creating fictitious characters to enhance the salability of their records. Mos Def says, "Why are the East Side Boyz' names Big Sam and [Lil] Bo? ... What's next, Kunta and Kinte?"[51] Clearly, hip-hop music's priorities have been weighed on the scales and been found wanting.

Chapter  Two

CHAPTER TWO (AGE): PSYCHOLOGICAL MANIPULATION BEHIND THE SCENES IN THE RECORDING STUDIO

What I see as being the major challenge that these kids will deal with is the image of young, urban America. Young people need to ask themselves, 'Who will control their identity?'[52]

—*Dr. Irvin*

"… what hip-hop has done is captivated the children … because we control the kids' mindstate"[53]

—*Ja Rule*

The Willie Lynch Letter is quite tenacious in its opinion to use age as a weapon to keep Blacks psychologically enslaved. In light of it, Ja Rule charges that hip-hop captivates and controls the youth's state of mind. This control started in the 1990s when youth born in 1973 and thereafter had gangsta rap targeting them. According to Chuck D, "From 1979 to 1992, there was a sheer abandonment [of rap music by Black radio programmers]. They banned it."[54] *The Black Commentator* adds that

> During that period, hip-hop broke out of the neighbor-
> hoods and fueled the founding of a host of independent
> (mostly white-owned) record labels—an explosion of
> musical creativity and social commentary of all kinds.
> But not until the early Nineties, after mega-corporations
> moved to swallow up the genre, did Black-programmed
> radio embrace the music of Black youth. In one of the
> great ironies of African-American cultural history, Black
> radio finally embraced hip-hop in the early Nineties—
> precisely when the huge corporate record labels shifted
> to gangsta rap. Industry researchers discovered that
> hip-hop's most 'active' consumer base was composed of
> 12- and 13-year olds—tweens—a cohort that is drawn to
> repetitive profanity and, not having reached the sexual
> pairing-off stage of development, revels in misogyny.
> Artists and recordings (A & R) executives put great
> pressure on rap acts to become more 'real'—a word
> that became a euphemism for egregiously profane and
> abusive language. In no time at all, the industry began
> churning out music geared primarily to younger juve-
> niles. Black radio, which had had such a problem with
> [rap] before the corporate-guided ascendance of gangsta
> rap, dived into the cesspool with wild enthusiasm. The
> airwaves became filled with edits, bleeps, and audio
> interruptions that did nothing to hide the 'denigrating'
> content. Black middle-class propriety was trumped by
> the servile imperative to follow the (White) corporate

leader. No one can measure the accumulated arrested development afflicting youngsters raised on a profane corporate formula designed for tweens.[55]

The figure below presents the musical themes within songs by some Black artists:

Figure 2.1 General Black Musical Themes

General Black Musical Themes Pre–1990	General Black Musical Themes Post–1990
<ul><li>Romancing/ Faithfulness in Relationships</li><li>Uplifting Blacks</li><li>Speaking against Injustice</li><li>Appealing to the Masses</li><li>Effecting Mood Positively</li><li>Fun/Dissing</li><li>Socially Conscious (Civil Rights)</li></ul>	<ul><li>The ho and bitch is more esteemed than the Black female</li><li>Females are not to be trusted</li><li>Females are referenced in relation to their body parts</li><li>Songs that are condescending to the race</li><li>Lyrics that are negatively risqué and, shocking, and that set trends (fashion or linguistic)</li><li>Hip-hop emulates what manhood is and the kind of men women desire</li></ul>

Black Hip-Hop Artists and Crime

Holley asserts "Today, district attorneys and prosecutors get especially anxious when famous rappers get charged by the police. Bringing them to trial is a no-lose situation: [hip-hop artists] are young, famous, and most importantly, Black. There is supposed to be a presumption of innocence when the accused go to trial. But when you are a young person of color, that all goes out the window."[56]

A former inmate wrote a letter that explains his turbulent relationship with hip-hop music. He writes:

September 29, 2005

Dear Hip-Hop,
It's been a long time hasn't it? We have both changed and endured so much over the years, but no matter what, I've always stayed loyal to you. I have endured three-and-a-half years of incarceration, and through my own trials and tribulations while inside, I've had a chance to look at the big picture and see you from a different perspective.

Hip-Hop, you have gone through a transformation since the days of old when you used to encourage unity, community awareness, education, and Black empowerment. Now you are overrun with corporate suits and more concerned with marketability and sales than your quality.

Hip-Hop, it seems like you sold yourself to big business, and now I have no choice but to search up and down the dial for that music that was once you. I know that Hip-Hop is an expression of what's happening within our communities and generations, but through that expression over the years you have allowed people to portray unrealistic and negative images to our youth and society.

It's painfully evident that the 'underground' has been abandoned by the airwaves. The mainstream is dominated by big names and labels, making it hard for the newcomers to break through.

At the same time, I don't want to seem like I'm ungrateful for the many years of great experiences that I've shared with you. Because truth be told, you helped me get through the many long days and nights within the belly of the beast. You were my therapy, a soothing calm that comforted me when I was stressed by the discomfort of being incarcerated. I couldn't have done it without you. Late at night I'd catch Emilio Sparks's underground showcase on the [College of] Staten Island's WSIA radio station and try to zone out until my release date.

During my incarceration, I encountered many young men who imitated facades that you can find in a music video. I've seen many men return to prison as a result of chasing the almighty dollar because of the depiction of the 'hustler' in music videos. It's mostly the younger men who are imprisoned that idolize the lifestyles that are glamorized on TV. I've even come across corrections officers that imitated the video personality and idolize the lifestyle.

You, Hip-Hop, are made for daily conversation. You are definitely an influential force. I use you like I'd use a pen, a tool that won't let the detours of life overwhelm me.

For every action, there is a reaction, and for every cause there is an effect. You may have forgotten, but your mouthpiece is powerful. That's why we all must practice making wise and conscious choices before we execute any action.

Time has changed both you and I, but no matter what, I still love you.

Love Always,
Mike

P.S. KEEP IT REAL[57]

Mike's letter exposes his tumultuous relationship with hip-hop in a voice that combines teenage petulance and adult maturity. He has witnessed young Black males returning to prison after mirroring the same criminalizing behavior they have seen in unconscious hip-hop videos. Hip-hop is being used as a form of advertisement to attract young Black males to fill the prisons. Consider this: "The prison-industrial complex has made people into financial assets. For every successful [hip-hop artist], there's 10,000 kids in prison who tried to follow what they heard on their album. The [artist] doesn't go to jail. It doesn't cost him anything to say it. But look what it cost the kid who tries to live it out. He's worth $25,000 yearly in state prison, $60,000 in super-max prison. ... It took 135 years for them to bring slavery back on the backs of our youths."[58]

This idea is reflected in the way oppressed Blacks feel an irresistible attraction towards patriarchy and its way of life: "Sharing this way of life becomes an overpowering aspiration. In their alienation, the oppressed want at any cost to resemble the oppressors, to imitate them, to follow them."[59]

Black Girls and Hip-Hop's Effects

Ying Yang Twins's "Wait (Whisper Song) which contains the lyrics "Just wait til you see my dick": *Wait (Til You See My Dick)* appeals to prepubescent young girls. Some of these girls answer the call by throwing *Rainbow Parties* where girls put on various shades of lipstick in preparation for performing oral sex on boys' penises. By the time all of the girls have *performed*, the boys' penises will have more rainbows on them than a bag of Skittles. It gives a fresh new meaning behind *tasting the rainbow*.

Wingood's study[60] found that Black teen girls who viewed a lot of hip-hop videos are more likely to 1) get into trouble with the law; 2) take drugs; and 3) contract sexually transmitted diseases. The research spanned from 1996–1999. The participants of the research were 522 Black girls between the ages of 14 and 18. The researchers found that girls who watched more than 14 hours of hip-hop videos per week were three times as likely as other girls who watched less to have hit a teacher. Further, 41% of them developed a sexually transmitted disease compared to 33% who did not watch as many videos.

Having multiple sex partners may bring a sense of power to these women as they believe they have a special commodity. In actuality, Black women, have far less access to appropriate protection, tangible wealth, and power and have historically used sex to advance their in positions. And now Black girls as young as 10 are imitating what they see in hip-hop videos, possibly longing to become mere sex toys in the videos of the hip-hop boys.

Black Women Providing the Blueprint for Black Girls

While the Black woman is unfortunately becoming more synonymous with bitch, trick, and ho within hip-hop, some Black women are supporting the blasphemy that comes out of the mouths of Black male hip-hop artists. Phrases such as: *Black men are just genetically dogs; they are just sowing their wild oats* have crept dominantly into in the minds of women. From this morass, some of these women are quick to hug themselves with pleasure every time Black male hip-hop artists call them any condescending name. The patronizing smirk on the hip-hop artist's faces is lost on the Black woman, and yet some are quick to defend the Black males, quipping that *they are not talking about me* while she dances and imitates the video girls they aspire to mimic. It is good for Black women to stand by their men, but even the country singer Tammy Wynette—who sang "Stand by Your Man"—would have advised Black women: *If you cannot be the table cloth, then don't settle for being the dishrag.*

But the video girls in hip-hop are treated like an overused dishrag. The purpose of the video girl is to create a visual entertainment for onlookers observing their curvaceous bodies. With the creation of Nelly's Apple Bottom jeans, Mystikal's *Shake Yo Ass*, and other products—odes to the Black booty—a woman's derriere and/or breasts are held in high esteem over anything else about her. This was not an invention of the hip-hop artists but of White supremacy possibly dating further back from the experience of Sara Baartman, dubbed *The Hottentot Venus.*

Sara Baartman: A Twenty-Something-Year-Old

Sara Baartman, like hip-hop's video girls, earned pennies from her master who put her exceptionally buxom breasts and buttocks on display for Whites' entertainment. Sara Baartman was dubbed *The Hottentot Venus. Hottentot* was a name given to people with cattle. Sara was born in 1789 in Cape Town, South Africa. William

Dunlop, a British doctor, noticed how exceptionally voluptuous and buxom she was and persuaded her to travel to London, England with him. By her own on will, Sara went. Dunlop displayed her as a *scientific curiosity* and a *freak* and made much money from putting her on display, promising her some to share some of the profit. Whatever he paid her, *if he did at all*, was not enough to buy her freedom from the life she was living. She was lured into a life of objectification.

White men would travel far to watch Dunlop's display of Baartman's prominent derriere and large genitalia (which was described as resembling the skin that hangs from a turkey's throat). She was required to parade in the nude along a stage two feet high, led in a cage or on a leash by her keeper and exhibited like an endangered species. Dunlop ordered her to walk, stand, or sit on command. In 1814, she was taken to France. Once the French became exhausted with the Baartman show, Sara was forced into prostitution; she could not adapt to a foreign culture and climate, or the further abuse of her body. She died in 1816 at the age of 26, possibly of syphilis.

After her death, French scientist, George Cuvier made a plaster cast of her body, then removed her skeleton and preserved her sexual organs and brain. They were displayed in the Musee de l'Homme in Paris until as recently as 1985. Her remains finally returned to Cape Town in 2002. Baartman was celebrated for her body parts, not for her being a Black woman.

This historical fascination with the Black woman's body manifested itself in Black women being raped and objectified by White men. During the 1700s, Black women were exhibited as zoological curiosities for their full lips, buxomness, and curvaceous appeal. It fueled the sexual desire of White men who raped them. Sara's experience parallels the experience of the women on the cover of the November 29, 1993 issue of *Time* magazine featuring Snoop Dogg with women in doghouses, on leashes, and according to bell hooks an

> ass out presumably waiting to be fucked from behind. The positive music review of this album, written by Christopher John Farley, titled "Gangsta Rap, Doggystyle," makes no mention of sexism and misogyny, makes no reference to the cover. I wonder if a naked white female body had been inside the doghouse, presumably waiting to be fucked from behind, if *Time* would have reproduced an image of the cover along with their review. When I see the pornographic cartoon that graces the cover of *Doggystyle*, I do not think simply about the sexism and misogyny of young black men; I think about the sexist and misogynist politics of the powerful white adult men and women (and folks of color) who helped produce and market this album.[61]

Clearly, Black women's bodies are used for commercial gain much like they were when White plantation owners needed to impregnate Black women to produce more commercial gains for their property. However, the psychology of racism and sexism is quite pervasive in this society, for "the mechanism of projection frequently coincides with and is complemented by displacement. This is when the anxiety, frustration, or cause of misery, whether social or instinctual, is attributed to a person or object that is less threatening and more accessible than the real source. The classic example is the man who is mistreated or misunderstood by his boss at work, and then comes home to yell at his wife and beat his children. If is safe to express his anger against them. His hostility is displaced from its true source, which is too remote or powerful to be attacked."[62]

History is repeating itself with Black hip-hop artists exploiting Black women. Akon, a Sengalese-American hip-hop artist, simulated a rape scene on a 14-year old girl at a concert in Trinidad according to WorldNetDaily.com. The girl's legs were forced open on stage while Akon gyrated between them. He simulated various sexual positions with this girl, appearing only to get off her just as fast as he got on her once he received an auditory climax from the audience who vehemently cheered him on.

However, it is a clever tactic on the part of recording corporations to use psychological control to draw and hire only those Black hip-hop artists who agree to oppress other Blacks; it is a prima facie case of the oppressed becoming the oppressor: Black and White youth display learned behavior, acting out roles, perceptions, sayings, and edicts of some White-owned corporations under the guise of endorsement from Black hip-hop artists.

Chapter Three

CHAPTER THREE (INTELLIGENCE)
IGNORANCE BUTTRESSED BY ARROGANCE

> *... the Negro's mind has been brought under the control of his oppressor. The problem of holding the Negro down, therefore, is easily solved. When you control a man's thinking you do not have to worry about his action. You do not have to tell him not to stand here or go yonder. He will find his "proper place" and will stay in it.*[63]
> —Carter G. Woodson

> *Learning would spoil the best nigger in the world. It would forever unfit him to be a slave.*[64]
> —Master Auld

If Willie Lynch ever lived, he would be proud to witness how effective intelligence is as a tool to keep Black psychologically enslaved. Chuck D points out that

Black intellect is rarely projected from a Black view-point. Black comedy is. Black family life from a funny point of view is. Black athleticism is. Black style and dress are. It's countercultural. Intelligent Black people on television like Oprah Winfrey and Bill Cosby do us well. Unfortunately, for every Oprah or Bill Cosby, there are twenty-five people trying to tell a joke, a hundred and fifty people trying to sing, and thousands of people trying to dribble a basketball or score touchdowns and dance in the end zone. As Bill Cosby said, 'Get people from anywhere in the world and they'll have a negative view of the Black man, because of what they've seen in the media, not what they know.'[65]

The lack of Black intelligentsia reflected in the media serves as one of the plethora of reasons why hip-hop should propel itself with all of the tenets of rap and with all the grace it can muster. In hip-hop's shameless quest to toady to the idle rich recording corporations, artists will go to great lengths to *exhibit* acts of ignorance that buttresses their arrogance displayed lyrically and cinematically. The paucity of intelligence within hip-hop is reflected in the baggy pants as a style, the usage of *nigga,* and the perpetuation of stereotypes.

Baggy Pants and Prison

Baggy pants, *wifebeaters*, shoes without laces, and other styles are adopted by many Black youth; White youth have gotten into the act by imitating such styles. But these youth oftentimes do not know the historical significance behind what they wear and why they wear it. Youth from the 1950s through today allowed music to dictate what styles are *in* and which ones were *out*. And it was accepted without question. Part of the reason as Kelley notes

> All young people buy into the rebellion in general, as part of rebelling against parental authority. On one hand this amounts to a sort of vicarious emotional pimping that whites across the board engage in vis-à-vis blacks. For marketers who want to appeal to white teenagers they go through the black community and target the inner city and then the black middle class and then there's a rippling effect. If you don't target the hard-core, you don't get the suburbs.' In other words, blacks are unwitting trendsetters whose tastes and talents are observed, detailed, and crunched out as marketing tip points to music and fashion companies (aptly described by Malcolm Galdwell in his article "The Coolhunt" in *The New Yorker*, March 17, 1997). When blacks react to their environment it is taken up as a style by whites who have gotten it from an intermediary source, rappers, and music videos. This 'style', particularly the music, is seen as having the desired effect of boosting sales and thus it becomes the music that allows a rapper to get paid. The record company pushes the music to white markets and some rappers then feel the need to act out the scenarios they have created. Black and white youth style themselves as hardheads and act out the music they have heard, trying to authenticate themselves.[66]

Chuck D, a rap artist of *Public Enemy* fame notes that

> Black and White youths are purchasing *Black styles* and
> do not know that those looks are marketed by [clothing]
> designers, particularly sagging jeans which started in
> prison. Jails stopped issuing belts in the 1970s because
> inmates were hanging themselves with them. So if an in-
> mate who was 140 was issued a pair of extra large pants,
> there was no choice but to let them sag. The same thing
> with wearing sneakers with no shoelaces. That style also
> started in the jails. Shoelaces were not issued for the same
> reason as belts. So brothers in jail would not have either.
> Today you have companies getting rich off of that style,
> selling it in the malls and shops of mainstream America,
> with a white guy taking in the profits. That style was cre-
> ated by a circumstance our people had to deal with while
> locked up in a system that held us back.[67]

It is a clear paradox that "hip-hop's stereotypical fashion statement,
[baggy pants], comes from jail—[Black] men without freedom
providing the dress code for men with all the freedom and luxury
capital of the world."[68]

Nigga Versus Nigger Versus Wigger

Since the inception of the term *nigger* nearly 400 years ago, it has
always been associated negatively with anything having to do with
Blacks. In nearly the last twenty years, *nigger* morphed into *nigga*
due in part of to a marketing campaign to endorse the acceptance
of this term. The gangsta rap group, Niggaz with Attitude, made
the *n-word* a more infamous star than any member of the group.

This antic is nothing short of a self-fulfilling prophecy where young Blacks have heard of themselves being called—verbally or non-verbally—dumb, ignorant, and stupid. *Nigger* is the number one symbolic reminder of the oppression Blacks have faced since their arrival to in North America. And while some hip-hop artists vehemently support the usage of this term, despite thinking they are empowered to change the meaning, they must be reminded of Roger Taney's maxim given during the 1857 Dred Scott[iv] case: a Black has not rights that a White man is bound to respect.[69] Blatant disregard for the *niggah, niggra,* and *nigger* has been demonstrated historically in works such as *Amos 'n' Andy* and *Uncle Tom's Cabin.* Black unconscious hip-hop artists who advocate for its usage do not necessarily gain respect using it in the company of the Whites who buy hip-hop. Rather, it empowers some Whites through confirming what they may believe about Blacks. How is the term empowering Whites and Blacks to develop plans to eradicate poverty, address unequal housing, police brutality, drugs, HIV/AIDS, and prison incarcerations among Blacks in and out of the ghettoes? How does the term *nigga* empower Whites or Blacks to bring about positive change within communities? The term *nigga* has never been espoused within one Black movement because the people within the movement understood the power of language. I don't know what's worse: being called a *nigga* by White man or being called a *nigga* by a Black man.

Even more puzzling is that many Blacks of the hip-hop generation freely embrace derogatory remarks made to them by hip-hop artists who claim to be reinventing language. The powerful effort

---

iv   Dred Scott sued for his freedom since he was made free only for the Courts to enslave him again. Roger Taney was the judge in the case who noted that Blacks are not citizens of the United States and do not have a right to sue for freedom or anything else.

of the Black people defining themselves as niggers is an original but soul-searing idea. Hip-hop has manipulated collective consciousness of young Blacks and Whites into believing that this redefinition of *nigger* is part of a revolution. Russell Simmons suggested that "twenty years ago 'nigger' was self-defeating. When we say 'nigger' now it's very positive."[70] Some suggest that *nigga* has a different meaning than *nigger*.

In the choreopoem *A Real "Nigga" Show*, actor and playwright Robert Lee Hardy stated that the *Chappelle's Show* made the term *nigger* more open "because now, I hear White people calling each other niggers. I think Dave Chappelle said, 'OK, y'all [White people] called us this, but now, y'all some niggers too.'" Hardy added that *A Real "Nigga" Show* "exemplifies 'Black people taking something from nothing and making it something.'"[71] But what is this something? Even Dave Chappelle contends that while he used the term *nigga* frequently in his skits, he did more to empower the Whites behind his show economically than to expose them for how they really see Blacks.[72] It is a distortion of Black history because the derogatory term carried only one meaning regardless of the ever-evolving spelling variations. Whatever the case, much of the vocabulary used in hip-hop has been a potpourri of self-degradation, a boiling cauldron of conduct best avoided. Whenever it is articulated, nigger, niggah or nigga, the word conjures someone who has a Black or brown face. And now, a Black or brown-faced hip-hop artist is quick to spew the term.

For example, Davey D. recalled going to P. Diddy's "concert in San Jose and watching him get 15 thousand people to raise their middle finger and say *Fuck You Bitch*…Right afterward Lil' Kim came out and got everyone to yell *Fuck You Nigga*. The majority of that audience was non-Black. It sure was strange hearing a whole bunch of White and Asian kids, some as young as 10, yelling *Fuck You Nigga*."[73]

Russell Simmons alleges that "hip-hop is a worldwide cultural phenomena that transcends race and doesn't engage in racial slurs."[74] However, youth are reminded of how they are *niggas* every hour on the hour via the same hip-hop songs they may hear on their local radio station that which may be Black-operated but not Black-owned. While the *Imus controversy* curtailed the usage of the term played on radio, youth can turn to shows like BET's *106 and N Park* to learn lessons on how a *nigga* acts. It is part of a larger the marketing plan to keep Black psychological enslavement active.

Wiggas and Niggas: Where Is the Historical Context

One result of hip-hop's massive popularity is the birth of the *wigga*, an alleged White nigga who mimics Blackness in hip-hop dress, body language, speech, and dress. While the wigga is deemed by some as an imitation of musical art, others see the wigga as a 21st century form of minstrelsy.[75]

But many White and Black youth have no historical reference behind *nigga*. Minister Paul Scott adds:

> America is the great nigga production factory, having inherited the nigga fortune from its parents in Europe. And while some may argue that various industrial or agricultural products may be American's chief export; the real chief export is *niggas* as the American media has exported this image and effected policies in countries around the world based on this image. While some may point to electricity and the telephone as this country's great invention, the crown jewel of the White supremacy has been the creation of *tha nigga*. Since the European's first contact with African people, the ultimate goal was

to transform Kings and Queens into niggers, niggra's, nigga's or any other variation of the term. Whichever term that is used, the definition remains the same: a permanent underclass robbed of their culture, spirituality and power so much so that they will never present a serious threat to the [oppressive] power structure and the intensity of embedded self-hatred would be so strong that they would only be a threat to themselves. Although our African ancestors were not perfect it is safe to say that we were not nigga's until we came in contact with the European.[76]

But ironically, proponents of the usage *nigga* are quick to say: "The artist ain't talking about me. A *nigga* (bitch, ho, trick) can be anybody." Let's suppose that just 'anybody', such as say, members of Congress, teachers, or police officers, were to use the term to describe anybody, then the spotlight would be on these leaders regardless of what their intentions were. They would be called *racist*. Anytime the term is used should clearly remind us of what was said to and of our mothers, fathers, sisters, brothers, and extended family members from the inception of the word *nigga* to the present. It is a conundrum how some Black hip-hop artists can be in support of gratuitous usage of racist and sexist language under the guise of *keepin' it real*.

Ignorance Is Bliss: Perpetuation of Stereotypes by Blacks

If we examined stereotypes surrounding Blacks, we can find it demonstrated can be found in some much of hip-hop music. If we looked for the *hoochie*, we can find her in the late-1990s song by B Rock and The Bizz "That's Just My Baby Daddy." If we looked for the *bitch*, we can find her in Ludacris' "Move Bitch Get Out the Way." If we looked for the *sex-craved male*, we can find him in Black Jesus' "What that Thing Smell Like" where the finger is barometer to determine just how fresh a woman's vagina is. If we looked for the *dominatrix*, we can find her in Khia's "My Neck, My Back, Lick My Pussy, and My Crack." If we wanted a *fried chicken specialist*, no need to consult the Colonel Sanders. We can consult YouTube's Ms. Peachez's "Fry That Chicken." If we looked for *shuckin' and jivin'*, we can look to DJ Webstar and Young B's "Chicken Noodle Soup," whose lyrics about chicken and soda is accompanied by a dance craze that mirrors it.[77] If we looked for the chickenhead—a woman who lacks intelligence but depends on her great looks and sex appeal to get anything she wants—we can find her in Redman's "Chickenhead Convention." If we looked for the fellatio performer, we can find her in D4L's "Bobblehead." If we looked for the Black guy who picks up women with a line promising to showcase his penis, we can find him in Ying Yang Twins's "Whisper Song: Wait til You See My Dick."

The perpetuations of these stereotypic images by Black hip-hop artists is originated with and have been utilized by recording companies as a means of maintaining patriarchal superiority. Many Black socially unconscious hip-hop artists have become the buffoon par excellence, and the jargon behind the Black hip-hop artist is motivated by financial greed. It is a foray into all things stereotypically Black that keeps to the 'master' record companies glee.

It is amazing that what can be heard in any type of pornographic video can be heard and seen in a misogynistic hip-hop video. BET network execs found that people in their 20s were a consistent audience for these videos.[78] The young people do not understand how they fail to recognize the ways in which the hip-hop lyrics they quote are really infiltrating their lives.

It is no surprise that corporations are commodifying hip-hop. Chuck D adds: "If you checked out the news lately, McDonald's offers a king's ransom to any hip-hop artist who is able to put Big Mac into a song. MTV—and more to the point, Viacom—is succeeding in extending a teenage life to twenty-nine or even thirty-one year olds. It is about extending this market and removing any intelligent substance in the music. Why would twenty-six-year-old 'teenagers' care about political ramifications if their backs are not up against the wall?"[79]

And why would some thirteen-year-old teenagers care about reading, making good grades, becoming goal-oriented, and wearing their pants upon their buttocks since intelligence is not a theme within derogatory hip-hop music? Admittedly, it is not hip-hop music's responsibility to train these teens on the importance of education. But hip-hop as a cultural phenomenon influences youth's behavior, controls their *mind state* according to Ja Rule, determines what clothing they wear, provides a lexicon of phrases, advertises how women should be treated, advertises how boys should act, among several other things. Why do we not see a showcasing of hip-hop music including education as a theme to help youth empower themselves? Even hip-hop knows that if the youth—Black and White—would become avid readers, the more they have a greater chance of discovering how they may be misrepresented in hip-hop.

Disregard for learning among some Black youth serves as *part* of the reason why an academic achievement gap exists between Blacks and Whites. These Black youth have been socialized into believing the more ignorant you are, the more *Black* you are. However, if you are a Black male who desires to be responsible,

wear pants that fit, and make good grades, you are deemed as acting White and not being *down* with the Black people. This psychological manipulation has influenced young Blacks aged anywhere
from 5–35 to remain in jails, ghettos, and prisons, and often means
they are often unable to improve their status since it is difficult for
a felon to get a job or vote.

What Do Names Mean?

Such ignorance has even translated into what hip-hop stars call
themselves. Maybe it is another way of redefining themselves, but
dictionary.com gives the worldwide accepted definition of what
the hip-hop artists' names mean.

Nelly: an offensive term for an effeminate homosexual male
Ludacris (ludicrous): causing laughter because of absurdity; provoking or deserving derision; ridiculous; laughable
Sam and Bo (the adoptive names of the East Side boyz): a disparaging term for a Black person
(Snoop) Dogg (dog): something worthless or of extremely poor quality; a despicable man or youth
Canibus: (Cannabis): any of the various parts of the plant from which hashish, marijuana, and similar mildly hallucinogenic drugs are prepared
Sticky Fingaz: a person who is subject to steal
Jim Jones: a preacher and founder of the Peoples Temple group who commandeered their mass suicide by poison; over 900 people died

And the list goes on. These artists' records are pitched to youth who
witness a monolithic view of the artist. The names are negative; the

lyrics are degrading; and the videos are bordering on obscene. And yet hip-hop does not hold itself liable for the behavior children imitate.

Chapter Four

CHAPTER FOUR (SIZE OF PLANTATION) SHORING UP THE BIG BUCKS AND SUBURBANITE LISTENERSHIP

> *"It is useful to think of misogyny as a field that must be labored in and maintained both to sustain patriarchy but also to serve as an ideological anti-feminist backlash. And what better group to labor on this 'plantation' than young black men."*
>
> *—bell hooks[80]*

Feminist intellectual bell hooks adds that "When young Black males labor in the plantations of misogyny and sexism to produce [hip-hop music], their right to speak this violence and be materially rewarded is extended to them by White supremacist capitalist patriarchy."[81] During the days of slavery, the Black male was often the source of entertainment for White overseers. These overseers would have the Black males compete against each other in various sports in exchange for better treatment, better quality second-hand clothing, better food, and/or their freedom. The competition could lead to bloodshed between the Blacks all for the economic benefit of Whites who placed bets on their favorite gladiator. Frederick Douglass watched these Black males engage in such psychologically destructive combat and charged "only those wild and low sports peculiar to semi-civilized people were encouraged."[82]

In this hegemony, plantations are the White-owned corporations while the slaves are the hip-hop artists. Black artists are often colonized by the White-owned record and/or distribution company, but this colonization makes the artist a *thousandaire* in comparison to the millions the corporation receives. These corporations were built from the ground up by taking advantage of naïve Black artists. It is a prima facie case of slavery reformed. But slavery—in any form—cannot be reformed; it must be dismantled at its root. Even the former Bush Administration, according to Chuck D, is trying to co-opt hip-hop for war. He explains:

> The powers that be are trying to meld, shape, and corral the culture of hip-hop into another speaking voice for the government. They have exploited hip-hop and some of the culture around it—magazines, videos, etc.—to recruit people into the military. The Army says it will give out Hummers, platinum teeth, or whatever to those that actually join. Early on in the recent war, *Vibe* magazine was working with the Army to recruit Black youth. They are willing to do this because they will take money from the highest bidder.[83]

Hip-hop is used to promote their plantations. Van Silk stated that the young uneducated Black artist believes that he is just a Black man making money.[84] But in reality, Silk says, the Black rappers are the slaves "making money for the MASTER … the record companies which [are] owned by corporations" (par. 16). Silk adds that all of these Black rappers are getting a loan in which

1.   They have to pay all the dough back.
2.   They record on a tape and must turn it in. It's called a master.
3.   Who they turn it over to, the record companies, are the slave masters.
4.   The artists or rapper will never own that master again, even if they sell 10 million records.
5.   The record companies pay for the videos, and the artist has to pay it back to the record companies (who own those masters).

Hip-hop artist, Prodigal Son, knows about this structure firsthand. Currently, he says he is "stuck in a situation where [he] got other people choosing [his] songs. ... The artist found out long time ago that we wasn't really makin' no money off our albums."[85]

Hip-Hop's Marketing Power

Hip-hop artists have seen criminality and hypersexuality sell millions, ignoring rap's beginnings of attacking the status quo. Now these hip-hop artists have become the status quo. The hip-hop artist cannot rebel against the Prince and then become the Prince.[86]

Courvoisier experienced astronomical sales "thanks in part to Busta Rhymes making the drink 'the hero of the song.' ... Talk about free advertising—no deal was struck between Busta and the distiller beforehand. And it is not even his favorite cognac." Hennessey is Busta Rhymes' cognac of choice, but this example is proof that; hip-hop artists "are keenly aware of their marketing power, yet they often aren't cashing in, choosing to rap the praises of their favorite brands for free."[87] Liquor companies target youth to increase their profits and use hip-hop artists to influence them (i.e. Rakim to promote Hennessey; Dr. Dre to promote Coors; and Lil' Jon to promote Cognac). Hip-hop magazines and videos are laden with liquor ads. While African-Americans make up 12% percent of the United States population, they purchase 38% of the liquor.[88]

To reiterate bell hooks notes, much of hip-hop is "part of the anti-feminist backlash that is the rage right now. When young black males labor in the plantations of misogyny and sexism to produce [hip-hop music], their right to speak this violence and be materially reward is extended to them by white supremacist capitalist patriarchy. Far from being an expression of their 'manhood,' it is an expression of their own subjugation and humiliation by more powerful, less visible forces of patriarchal gangsterism. … The tragedy for young black males is that they are so easily dunned by a vision of manhood that can only lead to their destruction."[89]

Na'im Akbar (2001) in *Visions for Black Men* posits that Black males' true nature:

> is not a nature of self-destruction. One of the problems with the many, many, many negative stories that can be told about us is the temptation to begin to believe that our deviance is our norm. It is very easy to begin to believe that, because we have serious problems now, that this is our nature. It's very easy to believe that black-on-black homicide is the nature of the black psyche. It's easy to believe that the abuse of drugs is the nature of black men, that the failure of black boys after the fourth grade

is the nature of black men. It begins to make us accept the deviance as the norm.

When hip-hop artists advertise to kill *niggas*, pimp *bitches*, smoke *weed* or *blunts*, and/or to drink *liquor* in the spirit of *reppin' da hood*, they have begun to accept that it is their nature to exercise criminalizing behavior. Their listeners may not realize that ignorance, pimping, consuming illegal drugs, and drinking liquor in excess could lead them and their followers on a path to incarceration. The more this ideology becomes a part of mainstream media, the more Whites believe that more Blacks live in the hood when it is only one in five Black people live in the ghettos.[90]

Prison: A 21st Century Plantation?

The United States' economic success is largely due to the free slave labor of Black people in the early days, but also cheap prison labor that has added millions to the coffers of corporations. Congress granted private companies access to prisoner workers through the Prison Industry Enhancement certification program. This program creation made cheap labor more appetizing considering it held the guarantee of mandatory sentencing. Further, there is no need for such companies to take payroll, vacation time, unemployment compensation, minimum wages, and human rights into consideration.[91] Further, prisoners may work for 4 to 12 cents an hour which is less expensive than paying Mexican and Taiwanese persons the already-exploitative rate of 60 cents per hour.

While much of hip-hop music glorifies criminal behavior, more young African-American males are entering prisons it in droves. And while it is the case, we cannot blame hip-hop for the fact that Black males are incarcerated at more astronomical rates today than ever before in American history. Kunjufu points out, "The government passed a Gangbusters bill which increases jail time and encourages the death penalty."[92] Unfortunately, many of the youth do not see is the parallels of between privatization and prison labor: "the majority of the inmates in question are Black or brown-skinned people; in some cases, private prison laborers are accompanied by a guard or overseer; the jobs of free laborers are accompanied by a guard or overseer; the jobs of free laborers are threatened by prison laborers as their wage significantly undercuts the minimum wage; and the wave of the future seems to suggest that private prisons will hire out laborers in the same way that plantation owners hired out slaves."[93]

The influx of Black and brown-skinned males arriving in prison daily gives them another obstacle to overcome: how to protect self. Khalil W., a former twenty-something-year-old prisoner indicated that his experience in prison was one based upon survival being because of his relatively small stature at 5'10" and 185 lbs.[94] He admitted to witnessing how younger males were often prey for seasoned males. The seasoned male would arrange for the younger male to be approached by other males interested in copulating. The seasoned male would come to defend the younger one, then after the skirmish is over, the younger one male, being naïve, scared, and inexperienced to the world of prison, has to pay the debt of protection via sexual favors and oftentimes performing domestic services for the seasoned one. Khalil adds that there is a parallel between the gangs in prison and the gangs out of prison. He stated that oftentimes frequently males join gangs in prison to increase protection.

And while the invincible hypermasculine image is particularly pervasive in hip-hop prison-themed videos, Joanne Mariner,

Human Rights Watch attorney and activist, reports that prison rape is common:

> In December 2000, the *Prison Journal* published a study of inmates in seven men's prison facilities in four states. It found that 21 percent of the inmates had experienced at least one episode of pressured or forced sexual contact since being incarcerated, and nearly one out of ten had been raped. ... An earlier study of the Nebraska prison system produced similar findings, with 22 percent of male inmates reporting that they had been pressured or forced to have sexual contact against their will while incarcerated. Of these, over 50 percent had submitted to forced anal sex at least once.[95]

Mariner has over one thousand letters about rape from young male prison inmates. There are 300,000 men who are victims of prison rape annually.[96] Roderick Johnson alleged he was a victim of prison sexual abuse. While incarcerated at the James A. Allerd Unit in Texas, Johnson stated he was raped by more than 100 men each day for 18 months. He sought help from prison officials who told him to "fight or fuck."[97]

With the glorification of thug life and criminal activity, more youth are falling prey to such behavior. Saigon, an up-and-coming hip-hop artist, stated that hip-hop music glorifies "... jail. It's not a celebration or rite of passage but something [that's] destroying us. ... By putting music videos out with Meagan Good visiting [you in jail], young kids think jail's not that bad. That's not reality. Reality is a grown man looking up your anal cavity. They don't show images of people getting stabbed, getting killed and the corrections officers killing people. They just show one image. ... Being in jail is like being dead. People who should care disappear out your life. ... And that's another thing they don't show in the videos. ... I did a long time in jail. In the beginning of my bid, I did all the wild and crazy shit, but by the middle of it I smartened up. I started to read. ..."[98]

Drama, known for the military-induced hit *Left, Right, Left,* says of his experience in prison: "When I got locked, it's like everybody that was there is gone. I haven't talked to my mom since I've been away. I get a visitor every now and then, but I'm way out in the boondocks. I spend most of my time in that cell, working on my autobiography, writing my raps. I got my GED and I'm expanding my vocabulary. ... Before I took that road of [armed robbery], I went through all the avenues that I could to get the money I needed for my business. I can't get no job. I didn't have no GED. I'm a convicted felon. Who gon' hire a convicted felon?[99]

Mysonne Linen was close to releasing his debut album in 1999 on Def Jam Records when he was convicted of a pair of armed robberies that earned him a seven-to-fourteen year bid. ... He says, "A lot of inmates say, "I remember you. You was on the Ruff Ryders album [Ryde or Die Vol. 1]. That was my favorite verse!" I'm trying to explain to them, This is just music. You can't live your life based on what's in a song. ... [Jail] isn't a place for anyone. Older heads used to make us think jail was the place to go. They glorified it. They didn't give us the truth. They didn't let us know: You miserable. You don't have no authority over your own life. You gotta come off a visit and have a man strip search you, look inside your rectum."[100]

Tab Virgil, aka Turk, gained fame in the late 1990s as a member of Cash Money Records' platinum super-group the Hot Boys. Being incarcerated for 16 months, he says that while being in jail: "I write. I read a lot—Black history books or maybe read the dictionary.

... They got drugs everywhere. ..."[101] It's an interesting statement considering that 60% percent of inmate crimes are drug related and that the typical characteristics of inmates are: fatherless, do not attend church (or religious worship), high school dropouts, and hang out on street corners from 10p.m. to 3a.m.[102]

But with an estimated one in three Black males trekking to prison, hip-hop *appears* to be key voices of recruitment. This method of false advertising is unconscionable, for they do neglect to tell the down side of the harsh realities of prison.

In prison parlance, the baggier your pants, the more it attracts another male. While many hip-hop artists don such fashions, they have their songs lyrics and attitudes exhibiting highest forms of homophobia. But Stoltenberg poses:

> Imagine this country without homophobia: There would be a woman raped every three minutes and a man raped every three minutes. Homophobia keeps that statistic at a manageable level. The system is not fool-proof. It breaks down, for instance, in prison and in childhood— when men and boys are often subject to the same sexual terrorism that women live with almost all the time. But for the most part homophobia serves male supremacy by keeping males who act like real men safe from sexual assault.[103]

But with more pseudo-lesbian scenes in some hip-hop videos, it begs the question: do such scenes provide a visual of just how comfortable he is with his sexuality or is it a mirror of how comfortable he wishes he could be with his sexuality? For "when a person has strong doubts about his ethnic, sexual, vocational, social, national, or personal identity, he may unconsciously adopt prejudice against others to compensate for a lack of certainty about who or what he is."[104] It may serve as the impetus for more hip-hop magazines displaying ads for men to meet men in their classified sections. The root of it, from one person's point of view, begins with hip-hop artists

> telling women to 'show me what you're working with' or listing all the defiling things that are going to be done to them once they do show what they're working with. By the time a boy reaches 18, he is already desensitized to both the sexual act and the feelings of women. It's no wonder that as our men become sexually desensitized, it takes more to stimulate them physically. How many times can you watch a thrusting pelvis before it stops having any meaning? They start to crave sex that may be a bit more risky and a lot more lewd as the ante is upped on what will satisfy them.[105]

Translating the Glamorization of Prison

An African-American man spent 20 years in prison for a crime he did not commit, but he was later cleared of the charges. He admits that "the prison culture is one of manipulation and control. A major part of surviving is to make the prison lifestyle a part of you. I know of straight guys who became other dudes *wifey* for protection. They started to enjoy it and act out roles; one of my boys who was just released found it very difficult to go back to wanting sex with only women."[106] In the spirit of having gaining and maintaining control, some male prisoners are subject to rape by heterosexual, bisexual, and homosexual males, thus relegating them to a sexually passive role. And once they are raped, "they are, for all practical purposes, slaves and can be sold, traded, and rented or loaned out at the whim of their 'Daddy.' The most extreme forms of such slavery ... are found in the maximum-security institutions and in some jails."[107] Some of the perpetrators charge that penetrative sex is psychologically heterosexual and "insist that the difference between the experience of entering a female mouth and of entering a male mouth is not significant, that the experiential difference between entering a vagina or female anus and a male anus is not significant. In all of these cases, they are aggressive, thrusting, dominating, stimulating the nerves in their own penis"[108] as a symbol of the victim becoming the victor.

But these stories are not remotely implied within hip-hop. Figure 4.1 provides some correlations between hip-hop and prisons.

Figure 4.1 Correlations Between Hip-hop and Prisons

In the World of Prison	In the World of Hip-Hop
Baggy Pants (due to oversized Uniforms)	Baggy Pants (marketed by White and Black fashion designers)
Don't Snitch as a code rule; it is better to become a victim than tell who the victimizer is	*Don't Snitch* as a code rule; it is better to become a victim than tell who the victimizer is
Heavily controlled by White officials but heavily inhabited by Blacks	Heavily controlled by Whites but heavily influenced by Blacks
No loose shoe strings to prevent possible hangings	No loose shoe strings as a style

Figure 4.1 Correlations Between Hip-hop and Prisons
(Continued)

In the World of Prison	In the World of Hip-Hop
Degradation of anything considered *feminine* (i.e. punks, queens) even though some male prisoners who rape other men in prison deem themselves straight	Degradation of women and anything considered associated with femininity(i.e. bitch, ho, slut, homosexual)
Act hard; don't show weaknesses; sell that image to other prisoners	Act hard; look hard in picture poses; sell such images to youth (who make up a large number of those incarcerated)
Many prisoners lack basic literacy skills	Lyrics are often written and articulated phonetically to portray the lack of basic literacy skills (niggaz, beeyatches, etc)
Congregate around others for protection; there's power in numbers	Congregate around others as a posse; in concerts, you see the hip-hop artist and his entourage
Relatively easy accessibility of drugs in prison	Accessibility of drugs as shown in videos; if they are consumed on the street, you can be sent to prison only to have your habit supported there

Figure 4.1 Correlations Between Hip-hop and Prisons (*Continued*)

In the World of Prison	In the World of Hip-Hop
Seek to convert men into submissive roles, reducing them to "females" where they have *pussies* not *assholes* and they wear *blouses* not *shirts*[109]	Seek to convert women into second-class citizens reducing them to body parts (i.e. "piece of ass", "pussy", "cunt", etc)
Being pimped by the prison system working for a little as 12 cents per hour with no benefits	Being pimped by corporate American record companies, oftentimes giving a mirage of wealth (i.e. a new artist throwing money in front of the camera, displaying mansions, expensive liquors, etc.) only for it all to return to its rightful owners
Teardrops tattooed denote gang affiliation, the number of persons the inmate killed, or the number of loved ones killed	Teardrops is more of a fad; in some cases, it denotes gang affiliation, the number of persons the inmate killed, or the number of loved ones killed

Jason Whitlock sums up how prison culture is being advertised, sold, and packaged to our youth. He says, "Prison culture is winning. It has corrupted a form of music that once gave us great joy and/or offered inspiration. Prison culture—with its BET and MTV videos, popular movies, acceptance in the mainstream media and false gods—Jay-Z, 50 Cent, Snoop Dogg—has perverted the American dream for black youth. The blueprint for black success painted by pop culture and the mainstream media goes something like this:

> **Step 1:** Four to five years posted up on the block building a small drug-dealing empire.
> **Step 2:** Three to four years shuffling in and out of prison on drug-trafficking charges.
> **Step 3:** Write and perform rap songs about dealing drugs, killing niggas, running from the police and bad-mouthing black women.
> **Step 4:** Sign with a major record label that is anxious to make money off prison culture.
> **Step 5:** Start your own record label and find other drug-dealers-turned-rappers or wannabe-drug-dealers-turned-rappers to exploit.
> **Step 6:** Buy a small percentage of a pro sports franchise, run around with NBA and NFL players and allow black and white members of the mainstream media to kiss your pinkie ring. ... Just like the prison system, hip-hop's popular music is another vehicle to imprison the minds and bodies of the youth who devour it."[110]

Prison and Drugs

As what appears to be a consolation prize for going to jail, some of our young Black hip-hop artists are provided with weed. Capone, the other half of C-N-N, stated, "… for all my jail niggas—when smoking in a stall, take a little baby powder. Squeeze it in the air. You inhale the weed and blow the weed in the toilet, and it'll suck the weed right out."[111] Hip-hop artist, The Game, add "You just feel more manly when you smoke blunts."[112] Manliness has been reduced to smoking blunts.

And speaking of this fascination with weed, it is the latest co-star in hip-hop's pornographic videos shown on BET or MTV. Snoop Dogg has become a spokesperson for *blunt wraps* according to TMZ.com.[113] But Mike Gray's *Drug Crazy: How We Got into This Mess and How We Can Get Out* points out:

> The media in the 1980s got hooked on the drug war itself. … A surveillance van with a hidden camera can park on a street in Harlem, but it has no access to the Chicago Yacht Club or the ladies' room at Dan Tana's in West Hollywood. As a result, the drug-war footage showing up as the nightly news focused almost exclusively on the urban street scene, and though the vast majority of drug users have always been white, the people doing drugs on TV were now black and Hispanic. When a couple of researchers from the University of Michigan spotted this phenomenon … [they] discovered that from 1985 onward, the number of whites shown using cocaine dropped by 60 percent, and the number of blacks rose by the same amount.

At the time of this writing, twelve percent of Black men ages 20 to 34 are incarcerated. While Black drug users and dealers behind bars are not *political* prisoners, they are imprisoned in hefty numbers and sentences for *political* reasons. Kunjufu adds that "sixty-two percent of all illegal drug users are White. Sixty four percent of drug convictions are Black and Hispanic." [114]

These incarcerated hip-hop artists' prison experience makes it quite clear that they are not *gangstas* as other hip-hop artists proclaim to be. While some of the incarcerated artists may *act hard* in around their *boyz in* front of the camera, they appear to be all smiles when posing with a White man. Chuck D adds:

> If we want to keep it real, it's hard as hell for a Black person to be a real gangster. We can play with the image of being a gangster or a player but we're not players and we're not gangsters. ... A gangster is somebody that can commit a crime, influence the law, and get away with it. ... Black people are definitely not a group immunized from law enforcement. They have not ever had that power in this country. [115]

As part of selling an image, hip-hop artists have to finesse what actions to portray in the media. For example, hip-hop artist 50 Cent made *The New York Press' 50 Most Loathsome New Yorkers* list, where he comes in at number 48 with this blurb:

> WHAT UP, GANGSTA? Look at you, up from the underground with mix tapes and DVDs in hand, riding the coattails of Jam Master Jay's murder into the TRL ether. We probably could have handled the *Teen People* cover, but the *Teen People* centerfold was off the cliff: You

posed in a bulletproof vest for a glossy magazine aimed at 12-year-old girls. Did you know that the press release for your Grammy performance had you next to Celine Dion and Richard Marx?

Reynard Blake asserts that "the brief excerpt shows the duality of the black artist: staying close to his or her base while expanding to reach larger (younger, white) audiences."[116] It is a case of the hip-hop artist trying to find a middle ground with between the snakes and worms.

Hip-Hop Patent on Poverty? Black Ancestral Survival

During a question-answer session of my presentation on this topic, I had a 21-year old Black male tell me: Rappers keep it real on how they lived and the hard times they went through. They got out of the ghetto through hip-hop music. So what if they sold drugs in order to survive? What would you do if you have had children to feed and you couldn't work?

My response was: Well, let's ask Clara Hale, who single-handedly raised 40 children and sent them to college and cared for over 600 drug-addicted babies. Let's ask Harriet Tubman who was dubbed Black Moses, who established the Underground Railroad where she freed her mother, father, brothers, sisters and over 300 slaves, who—in her last years in poverty—used her $20 monthly government pension to help establish a place for the elderly and needy. Let's ask Mary McLeod Bethune, who arrived in Daytona with only $1.50 to open a school that is now known as Bethune-Cookman College. Hip-hop artists don't own the patent for poverty. Our ancestors fared under far worse conditions and used education to get out. And they did not leave the race behind or say "Look at

what I got and you don't." So if a person has several children to
feed and cannot get a job but has a luxury car and decides to sell
drugs to make ends meet, then that person is disconnected with
Black history. Our ancestors provided the blueprint for survival
out of civil disobedience. Why sell drugs, parade as if your gains
are not ill-gotten, then get arrested, then get sentenced to 5- to -15
years for selling a bag of weed, only to have the very kids you are
claiming to support be brought up without you? Who is going to
take care of them then? Research your Black history to understand
the blueprint to surviving. There is nothing wrong with living
in the ghetto; but there is something wrong with staying there
generation-after-generation. If money is the only thing preventing
those in the ghetto from getting out, then it is time to re-evaluate
why there are more Lexus', Mercedes', and Jaguars in the ghetto
than in the suburbs.

This young man may not have made aware of the disconnection
between his history and hip-hop and how unconscious hip-hop
music may have shaped his mind. Many Africans would consider
living in the a North American ghetto is better than being raped,
better than not getting a meal a day, better than not ever sleep-
ing in a bed, better than having dirty water to drink, better than
watching hundreds of people die through war, famine, or disease,
better than being homeless, and better than not getting an education. Persons who adopt the young man's attitude should think
twice about the struggles of living in the ghettos rather than living
in African countries where some people wish they had access to
schools.

But as Tate argues, "if hip-hop had done nothing but put more
money in the hands of Black artists and business managers than
ever before, it would mark a milestone in American cultural history. What that wealth has not been able to transform, however,

is the social reality of substandard housing, medical care, and education that afflicts over half of all African-American children and accounts for as many as one out of three African-American males being under the control of the criminal justice system."[117] But in a valiant attempt to have a piece of what the oppressors have, the oppressed will become the oppressor. For example, Black hip-hop artists are among the oppressed; they become oppressors by denigration of the Black race in pursuit of money. For "money is the measure of all things, and profit is the primary goal. For the oppressors, what is worthwhile is to have more—always more— even at the cost of the oppressed having less or having nothing."[118] Any situation in which 'A' objectively exploits 'B' or hinders his and her pursuit of self-affirmation as a responsible person is one of oppression.[119] Clearly, the choices we make become who we are and what our destiny is.

Plantation Theory and Hip-hop

Chuck D, former rap artist for Public Enemy, developed the *Plantation Theory*. His theory posits that Blacks have clusters of plantations, not communities. A community, he contends, has control of the three E's within its environment: enforcement, education, and economics. Overall, Blacks do not have communities since there is White control over the plantation which tells Blacks that they are not permitted to employ themselves, write any laws, or educate themselves.[120] This theory translates into some hip-hop artists having an overseer who charges them to fill hip-hop music with "all kinds of negative, degenerative images. ... And that's exactly what's been happening. Negative is always easy to sell. If you give a fourteen-year-old a choice between a positive video, and a video with tits and ass, or guns and violence, he's going to choose the tits and ass, guns, and violence almost every time."[121]

As part of the plantation, some Black listeners of radio stations are listening to the same twenty songs, played in a row, throwing out phrases like, "Girl let me wax that ass with my ten-inch Johnson and feel yo' *breasesses*," and you have a ten-year-old prepubescent listening and the child does not get anything other messages communicated that different from that, "then what you have is a plantation that is run by somebody else's leash. Part of a radio station's responsibility is to serve the community with information. If it's not doing that then what its doing is purely exploitation."[122]

Such exploitation extends in the world of pimping. Youth growing up today listening to pimp-laden themes in hip-hop music and videos are influenced to mimic that same behavior advertised to them via hip-hop videos. Just ask the dubbed *tennis shoe pimps* who have roots directly tied to hip-hop culture. They consist of boys as young as twelve convincing girls around their ages to have sex with older boys and teenagers and give the money to them. If the girls want a piece of the money to buy clothes or anything of female interest, they can sell sex.[123] Maybe their pimping lessons started as young as first grade. A Biloxi, Mississippi first-grade teacher held a costume party where a boy dressed as a pimp complemented a girl costumed as a prostitute.[124]

Attracting young Blacks—males in particular—into pimping and drug using make it worthwhile for some politicians to advocate for expanding the prison system and spending less on education since young Blacks are entering into it in droves.

Chapter  Five

CHAPTER FIVE (EAST COAST VS. WEST COAST) A SHOWDOWN AT THE NOT-OK CORRAL

It used to be 'fight the power'; now it's 'watch what you say about me.'[125]

—*Mos Def*

One of the biggest tricks that's happening right now is our culture is being used to destroy us as a people because the negative aspects of it are being honed upon and magnified to the point where people think it's all entertainment.[126]

—*Chuck D*

The creation of distrust among Blacks has been paramount in keeping Blacks divided as a race. During the 1990s and 2000s, the media intensified this distrust with examples from the East Coast-West Coast conflict between hip-hop artists: on a war between East Coast artist mostly New York City and the West Coast artists from Los Angeles. In the mid-1990s, the East Coast was competing with the West Coast for control of the profitable hip-hop musical market. But on April 24, 2007, CNN's Anderson Cooper questions whether a hip-hop artists' feud with another hip-hop artist is decided by the record company to increase album sales.

The East Coast-West Coast warfare was an on-going barrage of public insults and nightclub skirmishes. This warfare even introduced the *East Coast West Coast Design* grills in platinum or gold. The hip-hop magazine, *XXL*, gives ten rules for beefing artists to play by to intensify the beef:

1. Shoot a low-budget video using video hoes than vixens;
2. Attack them in the media using subliminal or direct verbal jabs;
3. Create scathing t-shirts, preferably with slogans that openly disses the enemy;
4. Draw unflattering, funny illustrations;
5. Try to dismantle their crew using their weakest link;
6. Get their album pushed back or their budget frozen with the help of friends in high places;
7. Compare each other's soundscans and brag about who is outselling who;
8. Create a taunting catchphrase which can be a play off the other rapper's name or song;
9. Ban radio stations or DJs from playing the enemy's songs (if you have strong connections with the radio folk); and
10. Get the people involved using the hip-hop fans.[127]

The East Coast-West Coast hip-hop rivalry took place in the early to mid-1990s between East Coast's Bad Boy Records and West Coast's Death Row Records. The initial rivalry was between Bad

Boy Records' CEO Sean "Diddy" Combs and Death Row Records' CEO Suge Knight.

Diddy vs. Suge

Their tumultuous relationship began at The Source Awards in 1995 when Suge ridiculed Diddy in the company of rising artists and fellow record executives by stating: "Any artist out there that want to be an artist and stay a star, and don't have to worry about the executive producer trying to be all in the videos, all on the records, dancing, come to Death Row."[128] It was a jab on Diddy's presence on his artists' songs and videos. Diddy sought to assuage the matter. But it did not stop there. Dr. Dre and Snoop Dogg, hip-hop artists of Death Row performed later that evening and were booed. Snoop's replied: "The East Coast ain't got no love for Dr. Dre and Snoop Dogg and Death Row?"[129] Knight later went to Jermaine Dupri's party where one of Suge's closest friends was shot. Suge believed that Diddy may have had something to do with it.

Suge and Diddy were not the only ones allegedly engaged in an East-Coast–West-Coast battle. Tupac and the Notorious B.I.G, Jay-Z and Nas, as well as several others—as wikipedia.com[130] poignantly suggests—have been engaged in such battles.

EAST COAST

Participant	Based	Involvement
The Notorious B.I.G.	Brooklyn, New York	Once a friend of 2Pac, Shakur accused him and his crew of being involved in his 1994 shooting in New York, and proceeded to continually blast Biggie for the remainder of his life. Though Biggie never directly responded to 2Pac's repeated slants, he released tracks such as "Who Shot Ya?," "Long Kiss Goodnight," and "What's Beef," which many believed contain subliminal jabs at the rapper (though his camp denies this.)
Junior Mafia	Brooklyn, New York	Subsidiary act of The Notorious B.I.G., which included: Lil' Cease and Lil' Kim. All were slighted by 2Pac and The Outlawz. According to the Notorious B.I.G.'s *Behind The Music* profile, the members of Junior Mafia intended to record an answer song to 2Pac's insults, but were instructed not to by Biggie.
Mobb Deep	Queens, New York	A rap duo from Queens, New York. After having allegedly insulted 2Pac and his associates; 2Pac insulted them in interviews and on tracks. They later recorded an answer song, "Drop a Gem On 'Em." The duo also appeared on the song "LA, LA," a track in which Snoop Dogg and Tha Dogg Pound were slighted.
Capone-N-Noreaga	Queens, New York	Recorded the song "LA, LA" (which took jabs at Snoop Dogg and the Tha Dogg Pound) as in response to "New York, New York."
Nas	Queens, New York	A radio freestyle from Nas allegedly contained subliminal insults levied at 2Pac, who in turn insulted him on songs and in interviews. Claims now speculate that the two later settled their differences prior to the other rapper's death.

Participant	Based	Involvement
Jay-Z	Brooklyn, New York	An associate of The Notorious B.I.G., whose cameo appearance on Jay's song "Brooklyn's Finest" seemingly referenced 2Pac, who later insulted Jay-Z. Though he never publicly responded, Jay-Z later claimed that he had prepared a retaliatory song levied at 2pac, but didn't release it due to Shakur's death.
Common	Chicago, Illinois	Involved in a feud with West Coast rapper Ice Cube over his song "I Used To Love H.E.R.," which criticized the direction commercial hip-hop was taking—due to the influence of west-coast g-funk. Ice Cube jabbed Common on "Westside Slaughterhouse." Common responded to Ice Cube's insults with "The Bitch In Yoo." The two have since ended their feud and made peace.
DMX	Yonkers, New York	Became embroiled in a feud with rapper Kurupt over DMX's having slept with his one-time fiancé Foxy Brown. Kurupt insulted him on "Calling Out Names." DMX responded with "Bring Your Whole Crew." Their feud has since ended.

WEST COAST

Participant	Based	Involvement
2 Pac	Oakland, California	The east-west coastal rivalries most central and, arguably, most vocal figure. In the two years leading up to the his death, the rapper took potshots at various east coast rappers; most notably, The Notorious B.I.G.
Suge Knight	Los Angeles, California	Former C.E.O. of Death Row Records. His grudge against the success of the New York-based Bad Boy Records and its label head, Sean Combs, led him to sign 2Pac and (allegedly) encourage the coastal feud
The Outlawz	Essex County, New Jersey	New Jersey-based act, closely allied with 2Pac. The group often supported the rapper as he slandered his adversaries, and appeared on the infamous "Hit 'Em Up."
Tha Dogg Pound	Long Beach, California	A duo of rappers on the Death Row Records roster, who in 1996 released "New York, New York"—a track in which many New York emcees took to be a slight to their city.
Kurupt	Long Beach, California	Member of Tha Dogg Pound, who became involved in a dispute with east coast rapper DMX over allegations of DMX having slept with Foxy Brown. Kurupt insulted him on "Calling Out Names." Their feud has since ended.
Snoop Dogg	Long Beach, California	A former Death Row Records recording artist, who appeared with Tha Dogg Pound on the song "New York, New York." He also slighted Bronx rapper Tim Dog on the Dr. Dre's "Dre Day." Has since denounced coastal feuding in hip-hop, and has gone on to collaborate with other artists based outside of the west coast scene.

Participant	Based	Involvement
Ice Cube	Los Angeles, California	Became embroiled in a feud with Chicago-based rapper Common, after he denounced the themes of west coast gangsta rap in his song "I Used To Love H.E.R." Recorded the track "Westside Slaughterhouse" in response. Common answered back with the scalding track, "The Bitch In Yoo." The two have since made peace.
Westside Connection	Los Angeles, California	A supergroup consisting of west coast hip-hop rappers Ice Cube, Mack 10, and WC. Recorded "ALL The Critics In New York," and "West Up" in reaction to feeling that the east coast hip-hop community lacked respect for their coast.
DJ Quik	Compton, California	Quarreled with rapper Tim Dog for his tracks: "Fuck Compton," "DJ Quik Beat Down" and "Step To Me." DJ Quik responded on "Way 2 Fonky" and "The Last Word."

Chapter 6 Six

CHAPTER SIX (BLACK MEN VS. BLACK WOMEN) BLACK WOMEN ALONG FOR THE RIDE WITHOUT THEIR HANDS ON THE WHEEL

> *Rich corporations mass-market immorality (after all, they are the only ones who can), and then label their products as authentic representation of hip-hop generation morality.*
> —*The Black Commentator*[131]

Misogyny, sexism, and objectification have been thrust upon the minds of mainstreamed American culture since the days of slavery. Sexual exploitation is not only perpetuated by racy hip-hop lyrics and videos, but also it has the collaboration and consent of some women. It is these women choice to become contestants in hip-hop videos' *booty* pageants where the whole Black woman is never crowned winner, because of the "it-must-be-yo-ass-cause-it-ain't-yo-face"[132] mentality of the Black hip-hop. Many Black women have consented and collaborated in their own sexual exploitation. Their complicities support the notion that misogyny can even encourage "women to hate their own femaleness, an example of internalized oppression. The more women internalize misogynist images and attitudes, the harder it is to challenge male privilege or patriarchy as a system. In fact, women won't tend to see patriarchy as even problematic since the essence of self-hatred is to focus on the self as the sole cause of misery, including the self-hatred."[133] The pervasive images of Black women within hip-hop have become the false representation of all Black women. And youths around the world are buying into this misconception. Such ideology has become embedded in the psyche of youth and shaped their perception of the young Black woman as a sex-crazed, man-pleasing, morally irresponsible, and carefree person who has twenty children and is living off the government.

"I Wanna Light-Skin Chick": Hip-hop's Color-Caste System

Willie Lynch is adamant that color differences among Blacks are another means for controlling Black slaves by charging his fellow slavemasters to: "... use the dark skinned slaves versus the light skinned slaves ... whether they ... have coarse or fine hair."

Record producer and rapper Kanye West stated: "If it wasn't for race mixing, there'd be no video girls. Me and most of my friends like mutts a lot. Yeah, in the 'hood they call 'em mutts."[134] The *video girls* as poetically referenced by Kanye are a reflection of how the color-caste system is being reintroduced.

The color-caste system is another ominous aspect of corporate-controlled hip- hop. Bell hooks adds that dark-skinned females are not the desirable, sexy ones in the videos; in fact, the light-skinned females are desired. She posits, "The color-caste system is ... affirmed. It is rare to see darker females in rap videos. The lighter skin females are seen as viable and desirable. They are reinscribed as the most desireable."[135] It is clearly reflective of the premium Black—and White—men place on lighter-skinned, European featured, straight-haired, light-bright-almost-White women. Indicatively, the hip-hop artist exercises self-hatred against all things Black.

When unconscious hip-hop artists acquiesce to the wiles of record/distribution corporations, they create a rippling effect: the corporations exploit the artist, while the artist exploits Black women and themselves. The irony is that Black women's "attractiveness as sex objects to white men, singled them out for special exploitation and abuse under slavery. When a slave woman bore children, the children were automatically slaves and the owner's wealth expanded. ... Those who were light-skinned, were concubines for wealthy planters, gamblers, or businessmen; these 'fancy girls' sold for $5000, compared to $1600 for a prime field hand."[136] But "rather than punish or ostracize white men for such behavior, whites perpetuated a stereotype of Black women as sexually promiscuous and barred them from working alongside white women."[137] Black feminist writer bell hooks writes:

> Everywhere Black women went, on public streets, in shops, or at their places of work, they were accosted and subjected to obscene comments and even physical abuse at the hands of white men and women. ... A Black woman dressed tidy and clean, carrying herself in a dignified manner, was usually the object of mud-slinging by white men who ridiculed and mocked her self-improvement efforts.

Hooks also argues that Black women were channeled into urban prostitution.[138] "But now Black women were bad-mouthing them too. Books. TV talk shows. Newspaper articles. Movies. Everywhere they turned Black women were talking about them. The things they said about them sounded suspiciously like the same things many White men said about them." (Hutchinson p. 103) Hutchinson contends that one of America's dirty secrets is that most Americans fear and hate Black males yet are fascinated seeing them dance, tell a joke, sing, and play ball. This hatred also extends to the Black female. The racist stereotypes that pervade her is include being a goldigger—as reemphasized by Kanye West's hit of the same name—and violence-prone, a Jezebel, Delilah, and hypersexual.[139]

There is an apparent connection between corporate America's perspectives on Black men and how Black male hip-hop artists present themselves as misogynistic misanthropes on vinyl, disc, and video. For example, if the White man desires and sexually uses Black women, he "fantasizes and fears that black men will claim the same right and desire. Thus the white man who uses black women sexually perceives the black man as a menace to him and his women. By projection, the black man is seen as the one who lusts after white womanhood. This projection—'it is he, not I, who is lascivious'—is both guilt-evading and self-assuring because the evil doer who violates social morality is the other man, not oneself."[140]

It is part of patriarchy's deep roots. These stereotypes among others are played to the hilt in parts of the hip-hop world. For example, it is a reflection of America's clandestine fascination with, and shame surrounding, sex. Two examples: In the 1870s Anthony Comstock, a compulsive masturbator, became America's first spokesperson against porn. FBI chief J. Edgar Hoover not only collected a trove of pornography at the tax payer's expense but also dressed in women's clothing and cavorted with young men.[141]

Slaughter argues, "The macho image that Black men have of themselves is a distorted image that comes from a White supremacist male point of view. Since the days of being brought/bought to the U.S. as slaves, Black males have never had their own definition or model of being a Black man. Their original identity was lynched, castrated, beaten, and driven out of them. A new European macho image was forced upon them."[142] Many hip-hop artists have been reduced to some of its artists accepting pay to demean Black women and men in every way possible. 50 Cent has gotten in on the act by planning to make condoms and creating a vibrator that is a miniature motorized version of him.[143] Further, he has women on leashes in his P.I.M.P video. These females—often referred to as *extras*—are paid up to $100 for a 12- to 24 hour shoot if they are paid at all. The featured girls are those who get the most camera attention in the hip-hop videos. These video vixens are referred to as "top-shelf bitches" and can command as much as $3000 a shoot.[144] One former hip-hop video vixen better known as *Superhead* stated that "the top reason a woman finds herself in a [hip-hop] video, sprawled undressed over a luxury car while a rapper is saying lewd things about her, is a lack of self-esteem."[145] Another reason is a result of the sexist society we have inherited from patriarchy. Part of the damage this society has done to girls is convinced and conditioned them to believe that they deserve to be oppressed. And when she has been oppressed for a lengthy amount of time, she exhibits behavior indicative of the oppressed woman. Her psychosis at this point is to find satisfaction and justification in being objectified by the very men—Black, White, or other—who oppress her. For those hip-hop video girls, it is desirable to compete with women for the attention of a man. These video girls might have been spotted in Nelly's "Tip Drill" where one girl has her leg cocked high. Or you can find them in Ludacris' video where Luda's head is between the open, naked thighs of a woman who flexes her buttocks in his *Pussy Poppin'* video. These videos are savory to the eyes of Black Entertainment Television (BET) *Uncut* viewers where our young girls learn how to *pussy pop, booty clap,* and *drop it like it hot.* Our young boys and girls imitate what they see in these hip-hop videos evidenced in the styles, nuances, sayings, and verve they portray. And when our boys constantly see images of scantily clad women, it is they are more likely to objectify females. Girls will play the role by seeing themselves as a commodity, especially the more they imitate strippers. Something is definitely wrong when a young woman holds a stripper in higher esteem than such Black female heroines as Sojourner Truth, Mary McCloud Bethune, and Fannie Mae Hamer. These video strippers may consider themselves as *paid,* but Allan Johnson notes:

> Men who pay women to strip in front of them do far more than pay to watch someone they find beautiful or arousing take off her clothes. They also participate in a much wider social pattern that defines women's existence in relation to pleasing men, to meeting male standards of attractiveness, and to being available for men's appropriation and use. To some degree, the price of admission buys men the right to feel, if only in short-lived fantasy, a sense of indirect control over women's bodies. … the commercial exploitation of women's bodies isn't simply about social class and capitalism; it also involves a patriarchal system that normalizes and promotes sexual exploitation.[146]

Weddington asserts that "over time young Black girls are beginning to internalize what they see in the media."[147] Weddington's company conducted a study of thousands of Black teens from age 16 to 20 from low-socioeconomic backgrounds. They focused on ten cities across the United States, including New York, New Orleans, Chicago, and Los Angeles and asked the girls about sexuality, the media, and music videos. Weddington's analysis concluded: "The message young women are getting is that if they can't get something they want through their talent or ability, then they have something else that they can use, and that's their bodies. They are learning that what's important about a woman is her body, not her mind. So that means, 'I am a commodity, therefore I'm going to use that commodity to get what I want.'" She further argues that "when girls use their bodies as barter, they are more likely to engage in risky behavior like unsafe sex, sex with multiple partners or sex with men many years their senior."[148] "*BET Uncut* had been mostly under the radar until a 2003 video by the rapper Nelly went into the rotation. In 'Tip Drill', a song about a girl with an ugly face but a [curvaceous] body, throngs of women in bikinis swiveled their hips orgy-like by a swimming pool among fully dressed men. Grinning, the rapper capped off the video by swiping a credit card down the derriere of a comely woman. ... It netted her $1,500 for a day's work."[149]

It is a reflection of old White patriarchal ideology. The hip-hop male artists act "the role of the 'tough guy,' trying to appear hypermasculine. His conceptions of masculinity and femininity are exaggerated and rigid. Therefore he fears and rejects all that appears as soft, feminine, or weak."[150] Male youth throughout the world adopt such tenuous viewpoints on masculinity, not realizing that Black masculinity was stripped from African males when they were brought to North America. For over 400 years Black men have been attempting to salvage African masculinity, only to encounter confusion and doubt. And when a Black man "has strong doubts about his ethnic, sexual, vocational, social, national, or personal identity, he may unconsciously adopt prejudice against others to compensate for a lack of certainly about who or what he is."[151] This prejudice is lashed against the Black female who is complicit in her degradation because she allowed the monolithic images of video girls to teach her all she knows about femininity. This one-dimensional perspective of Black women is what she sees; but White women have multi-dimensional perspectives well represented in media.

Homosociality

Homosociality is the notion that all men—whether heterosexual, bisexual, or gay—are raised in American culture to be more eager to please other men than women.[152] For example, men hoot, whistle, stare lustfully at women, realizing that it may not actually work for picking up women. Through the lens of homosociality men stare, whistle, catcall, and hoot to connect with other men; even women serve for devices for creating same-gender, non-sexual bonds. Yet when these men are not around *the boys*, their behavior towards women is not nearly as pronounced.[153]

Through this lens of homosociality, it is common to see the Black male hip-hop artist and his posse conducting group objectification of the ass-shaking, pelvis-gyrating, *pussy*-popping women who are salivated over like a T-bone steak. Homosociality tells the larger society that these video girls want to service men in *every way possible* and because of such desire, they are nasty hos whose values lies only in the lower part of their bodies. They teach that women should be pimped and are never to be trusted. They teach that women should cater to their every whim, that women should be conquered, that women are second-class citizens, and that after the artist has used the woman, his boys can have immediate access to her.

Hopkins and Moore note that in "the commercial hip-hop lyrics themselves women enjoy a largely schizophrenic existence, primarily falling to the extremes of the age-old Madonna/whore split: Either 'My mama is the best in the whole wide world' or 'Bitch, eat my balls.' If rappers are modern-day blues singers or the Black CNN of the streets telling it like 'tis' from the streets, then it's fair to conclude that in the hood you'll find a deep hatred toward women. Considering the international popularity of hip-hop, make that a widespread hatred toward black women around the world."[154]

Misogynistic ideas and practices from slavery have been passed down to today's hip-hop youth. For example, during slavery Black women were often forced to have sexual relations with any slavemaster, overseer, or slave that desired her. In addition, these women were often used as instruments to produce more human property. From it emerged the stereotypes of the Black woman as a ho. Some hip-hop music still adopts the foolish ideology that there are two kinds of females in this country, colored women and white ladies, and the only time colored women become ladies is when they are cleaning ladies.[155]

But the most insidious form of racism and sexism is one that is hidden. During Reagan's presidency, the media provided descriptive rhetoric of Blacks camouflaged behind such terms: *crime-prone, gang-infested, ghetto outcasts, ghetto poverty syndrome,* and *drive-by shooters*. Since the early nineties, many young Black males do not call Black females *sister*; they call them *bitches* and *hos*. Many Black men don't call other Black men *brothers*; they call them *nigger*. Many Black women don't call black men *brother*;

they call them *dogs* and *bastards*. Many Black women don't call other Black women *friend* but *bitch* and *tramp*.[156] Such words carry connotations reflective of how the larger society views Blacks, no matter how strongly the microcosm seeks to redefine negatively ascribed terms and turn them into positive ones. The derogatory terms ascribed to Black women are not ascribed to White ones. Hutchinson notes that "Hollywood superstar madam Heidi Fleiss has how many Black females working for her? Most of the high-priced prostitutes are White. They don't ply their trade on the streets but in expensive salons and mansions. They rarely get busted because their clients are some of the richest, most powerful men in America. Unlike Black women, they don't call the women that service them whores or tramps, but madams, call girls, escorts, and professionals."[157] But the media—with the help of some hip-hop artists—make the public believe that more Blacks consume and sell the drugs. Sociologists talked to White and Black drug users and found that 93 percent of White male users were far more likely to sell drugs than 67 percent of Black male users. Heroin users were overwhelmingly White males.[158]

Such acts of self-depreciation are only an internal reflection of how the oppressors view them. Hence, if they hear that they are niggas, bastards, crime-prone, and hos, they will eventually believe it and act accordingly. What is even worse is how those who are being oppressed and exploited will defend the Black hip-hop artists' poetic license to degrade, denigrate, devalue, and eventually destroy our Black men and women. This cultural phenomenon is a boon to the Klu Klux Klan, who now have something in common with the Black Klu Klux Klan: they hate Blacks and the progress Blacks have made through the Civil Rights Movement.

Chapter 7 Seven

CHAPTER SEVEN (SLAVES WHO TRUST AND DEPEND ON US): VICTIMOLOGY AS A SPECTATOR'S SPORT

When referring to the 'power brokers' of Hip-Hop, right now the majority of them are white.[159]

John White's *Black Leadership in America: 1895–1968* quotes James Baldwin: "The moment one realizes that the real role of the Negro leader, in the eyes of the American Republic, was not to make the Negro a first-class citizen but to keep him content as a second-class one."[160] During slavery, overseers did not have to use leashes or guardrails to prevent slaves from escaping. They only used psychological tactics that kept slaves ignorant of their cultural backgrounds and the world outside them to the point where the slaves had to trust and depend on slaveholders. Our reality is constructed based upon what societal mediums—public school curriculum, police, advertising, hip-hop artists, parents, family—have told us. Youth of the hip-hop generation do not realize the ways in which institutional discrimination is an endemic part of their experience. Their ignorance is no accident.

While most hip-hop videos are replete with mansions, bevies of scantily clad women, expensive cars and jewelry, they pander to corporations who own the record labels and distribution of their music, which is the money-making nexus of hip-hop. A powerful White guy's bankroll gets heftier and heftier every time degrading images are used in videos or articulated in lyrics. A common physical description of many hip-hop artists is Black, male, and dark-skinned. These artists toddle a tightrope as they serve the corporation while trying to maintain their street credibility. If his street credibility is lost, the artist quickly loses White suburban males, which is, strangely, his consumer base.[161] So these artists have to exude a thug image to keep the bucks flowing.

Some hip-hop artists have loaned their names to corporations that disseminate explicit material. Amber points out that hip-hop artists are "now appearing in hard-core porn. In 2001 and 2003 the best-selling adult videos of the year were Snoop Dogg's *Doggystyle* and *Hustlaz: Diary of a Pimp*, respectively. Snoop acts as a tour guide in the graphic DVDs, featuring naked adult-film stars engaging in among other things, anal and group sex. ... Over the past several years, other top-selling rappers like 50 Cent, Lil John, and even old-schooler Ice-T, who currently stars on NBC's *Law & Order: SVU*, have hosted adult videos. Ice-T's top-selling project: *Pimpin' 101*, shows the rapper educating viewers on the different types of girls who work the streets."[162] In 2004, Lil' John and the East Side Boyz released an adult video entitled, *Lil John and the East Side Boyz American Sex Series* which includes a graphic girl-on-girl sex scene. 50 Cent and the dismantled group G-Unit released an interactive sex DVD entitled *Groupie Luv* that allows the viewers to select partners, sexual position, camera angles, and even the dispositions of the women ('naughty' or 'nice').[163]

And with all of this self-hatred being pronounced on Black culture, "somewhere in corporate America, someone is laughing at us—at how we degrade our own women and poorly influence our youth. We, African Americans, no longer have slave masters but have become slaves to ourselves through the hip-hop industry's recycling of the same ignorance and hate that brought us to this continent in the first place."[164] The hip-hop artists who are projecting degrading lyrics are the oppressed who have become the oppressors, and are rewarded with a few dollars to do so. Bowling notes that "Whites have followed Black culture's lead and they continue to do so. But if a group of White kids saw 50 Cent and his then G-Unit walking behind them on the street, those kids would be scared as if it was Jason wearing a hockey mask and carrying a chainsaw."[165]

As the oppressed continue to be the oppressors, the oppressed self-depreciates, "which derives from their internalization of the opinion the oppressors hold of them. So often that they hear that they are good for nothing, know nothing and are incapable of learning anything—that they are sick, lazy, and unproductive—that in the end they become convinced of their own unfitness."[166] Freire adds that "Indeed, the interests of the oppressors lie in changing the consciousness of the oppressed, not the situation which oppresses them; for the more the oppressed can be led to adapt to that situation, the more easily they can be dominated."[167] Mos Def points out that "it's starting to be like the corporations are only supportin' personalities and stories that fit into a perception that is easily digestible for them in their experience or a character that they're fixated with. People in control like to see niggas fighting, gangster posturing. Those are the only stories they're interested in. ... Unfortunately, [racism is so much] a part of the American psyche that people are acting out racist reflexes without realizing it ..."[168]

The experiences of artists like Snoop Dogg, Lil Jon and 50 Cent raise a pertinent question: Can persons be financially successful but still in bondage if they can be bought or sold at any cost?

Whose Really Getting' Paid in Hip-Hop Music

Kunjufu poses a few mathematical questions about the hip-hop business that merit answers. Question one: You sell one million CDs at $18.00. How much do you make? Answer: $18,000,000 possibly. Not a bad payoff for a hip-hop CD, but you have got to pay some folk. Question two: How much do the distributors earn? Answer: Distributors earn 50% of the $18,000,000. That's' $9,000,000, leaving you with $9,000,000. But you are not finished paying folk just yet. How much do the producers earn? Answer: Producers earn 40% of the $18,000,000. That's $7,200,000, leaving you with $1,800,000. Question three: How much do you owe in studio and video costs? You have to pay $800,000 which leaves you with $1,000,000. Uncle Sam's hand is extended for you to give him 40% of the $1,000,000 which is $400,000, leaving you with $600,000 ($1,000,000 minus $400,000). Then, you have to pay the four people in your group from the $600,000 remaining, leaving each member with $150,000. But only 4 percent of rap CDs achieve gold status (500,000) units.[169] It is no wonder record companies eye young Black hip-hop artists the way a glutton eyes a smorgasbord; they know that they can make an enormous amount of cash off their backs.

Religious Imagery and Hip-Hop Music

G. Craig Lewis reminds us of the religious influence hip-hop music has on the lives of its listeners. Snoop Dogg's 1994 *Murder Was the Case* DVD is one example of a hip-hop song sprinkled with religious ideology. The protagonist, Snoop, is shot; while he is dying, Satan appears to him bargaining that if he promises him his soul, he will not only bring him back to life but also make him rich and famous. Snoop agrees. A crow flies into the room which turns into a pseudo-Jesus who then turns into Satan while a church choir is singing the hook of the song. It was at that point that Calvin Broadus, Snoop Dogg's birth name, dies and Snoop Dogg is born.

Lewis asserts that hip-hop lyrics prophesy into youth's destinies every time the children recite them.[170] He relates it to how curses were pronounced on people during the Salem Witch trials. For example, Bone Thugs n Harmony's album E 1999 Eternal contains songs entitled, *Me Killa, Land of the Heartless, Die, Die, Die,* and *Mo Murda.* There is an Ouija on the back cover of the album that contains a lengthy message written backwards. Lewis posits that during Salem trials, witches sent curses in an envelope to people. The curses were written backwards; hence, people held them up in front of a mirror to read aloud, thereby speaking the curse into their lives. Words have power; life and death are in the power of the tongue. It is time that we begin reversing the curse.

Chapter 8 Eight

CHAPTER EIGHT (REVERSING THE CURSE: WHAT ALL OF US CAN BEGIN TO DO)

Yet I had planted you a noble vine, wholly a right seed: how then are you turned into the degenerate plant of a strange vine unto me? (Jeremiah 2:21)

"I believe what's happening in hip-hop now would be a disappointment to its founders, as it's so filled with ignorance and hate. It has done exactly what those who oppose this culture have always wanted it to do—enforce self-hatred among its people."
—Karrine Stephens aka Superhead[171]

Nothing will work unless you do.[172]
—Maya Angelou

Only an idiot won't change after they've learned something.[173]
—Kanye West

Daz Dillinger, cousin of Snoop Dogg and a hip-hop artist, charged that 21st plantations are destroying Black
people. He quips, "I am beginning to believe that slavery
is back. Everything is a plantation; whether you work downtown
or you work in a factory, we are still in a plantation. And just
because someone receives money doesn't mean they are free
especially if they are threatened to lose the money if they don't
do what they are told. This is slavery in 2006 and in 2007, and it
is my goal to make sure we escape and get free."[174] Part of his plan
to help free others is to take more responsibility for how his lyrics
affect children and to have his next release, *Dogg Chit*, mark the
last time he will use the term *nigga* since it is a reflection of a
"self-hatred mind frame."[175]

All hip-hop is not degrading, condescending, or destructive.
Thus, censoring hip-hop music is not what should be advocated.
What should be advocated is for Blacks to break the curse of self-
hatred. Why? Because this curse of self-hatred was "born out of
the Great Experiment (Racism), which many people believe was
successful. The Great Experiment begged the question: How do
you make a slave? How do you make a slave in perpetuity? You
make a slave for life. And you make the slave's children your slaves;
and their children, and so on. You make them *think* they are free, as
long as they hate themselves and fight amongst themselves."[176] It is
OUR responsibility to make a Herculean effort to begin changing
patriarchal attitudes, culture, and systems so that the generational
curse of misogyny over our women can be broken. Hip-hop is
becoming directionless and purposeless yet an integral part of
music history. The curse should be broken. Once it is broken, then
children who aspire to be hip-hop artists will not have a historical
basis to write derogatory lyrics.

Our ancestors lived, worked, fought, prayed, and died as a part of for the struggle to afford succeeding generations the opportunities to vote, read, obtain higher education, live in integrated areas, and celebrate Black History Month, among many other rights and freedoms. We have to ask ourselves: What are we doing with the knowledge they imparted to us? How can we ensure their fighting was not in vain? The Atlantic Ocean is the largest grave in the world, filled with the world's African ancestors who stood up to make our world better than they found it. They passed the torch to us entrusting that we too will make a positive difference in the lives of those that come after us. In some regard, the Black race is like an ostrich who escapes reality with its head in the ground, while its buttocks are being kicked by the rest of the world.[177]

Rap music in its heyday brought issues of police brutality, homelessness, poverty, and disenfranchisement plaguing the Black community to the forefront. The baton was passed to hip-hop music to address current issues surrounding Blacks: HIV/AIDS, high prison rates among Black men, drug usage, gangs, voting, political disenfranchisement, among others. These issues appear to be glamorized within hip-hop rather than hip-hop bringing the problematic issues to the forefront. Perhaps we should consult the words and actions of some of our ancestors.

The relationship between Black unconscious hip-hop artists and their White-owned record companies is analogous to the experience of the Israelites and the Egyptians from Exodus chapter one.[178] The Black hip-hop artists, like the children of Israel, filled the land with music and exceeded mightily in exposing the injustices faced by Blacks and Latinos in the form of rap, to prick the conscience of patriarchal America. But a new king of the Egyptians, money-hungry recording and distribution corporations, developed a plan to redirect the hip-hop artists; acting as taskmasters they provided a blueprint of the themes that hip-hop music should contain. And while the Israelites built treasure cities for Pharaoh, Black hip-hop artists are building empires for most White-owned record companies at their own culture's expense, by projecting an *image* that attempts to convince other Blacks that they are niggas, niggers, bitches, hos, and tricks, but that they should not allow people from other racial groups to refer to them as such since it would be considered racism. They project this image in videos where using guns to kill each other within Black communities is encouraged. But if a member of a White community kills a Black person—for whatever reason—we are quick to join forces and hold hands, remembering a modicum of our history by singing *We Shall Overcome*, not realizing that *we overcame.* Like the Egyptians' manipulation of the Israelites, White-owned record companies are having the children of Black hip-hop artists serve them with rigor. And in the midst of this subservience, the king of the Egyptians commanded to midwives that sons born to mothers should be killed, whereas daughters born should live. The 21st century Egyptian patriarchal record companies are commanding Black hip-hop artists to participate in killing young Black males en masse by fostering ignorance and a wanton disregard for Black history, by participating in criminal activity that leads to jail or prison life, and by blatantly disrespecting Black women while holding greater respect for White women, displayed by using the Whites' definition of beauty as exemplified in the proliferation of mostly, if not all, light-bright-almost-White girls in hip-hop videos. After all, *it-must-be-yo-ass-cause-it-ain't-yo-face*[179] attitude is the driving force behind a Black boy's belief growing up that disrespecting Black girls is an endemic part of Black masculinity. Along with this redefining of Black masculinity comes crotch-grabbing, baggy pants, baggy shirts, platinum teeth, ignorance, creating baby mama drama, directionless, jail and/or prison terms, being from the 'hood—whether you really grew up there or not is irrelevant; just act like you from the 'hood.

Much like Moses, who was appointed to call for the deliverance of the Israelites out of Egypt, Martin, Rosa, Al, C. Delores, Jews, Whites, abolitionists, and others were appointed to call for the deliverance of Blacks, socially conscious Whites, and others out of the land of racism, ignorance, and inequality created by patriarchy, who like Pharaoh, felt that Blacks were inferior and should serve patriarchal interests. Unfortunately, just after Martin was killed and the slogan *I'm Black and I'm proud* fostered Black pride, and rap music vehemently took up the torch to continue to fight against racism that progressively lead Blacks out of the land of Egypt—the land where we were fed with manna that empowered and enhanced race relations, where Black and White children played together regardless of color—the creation of *derogatory* hip-hop took Blacks back into the land of Egypt. This time record companies are providing a musical formula of that fosters patriarchy and racism. But while this Pharaoh is raking in the profits, Black hip-hop artists are spreading his message to the Israelite populace. Pharaoh is paying the hip-hop artists for providing the blueprint on how young Blacks should make excuses for why they want to be enslaved in ignorance; for why they should want to be bitches, tricks, hos, niggas, nigras, negresses, or niggers; for why they want to be psychologically enslaved by mimicking styles that stem from prison; for why they should not want to read, and for why they should be against other Blacks who are against denigrating hip-hop lyrics and videos. Pharaoh has done an excellent job of convincing these hip-hop artists that they deserve to be slaves; in turn, the artists are convincing young Blacks hip-hop listeners to do the same.

The White and Black *Moses* who are still with us will not be with us forever. It is North America's responsibility to take up the torch to be passed down; otherwise it will simply die out, burning their hands. Black America is in a state of decadence and needs to help raise young Moses' within its community to fulfill Martin Luther King Jr's dream. As previously stated, Martin Luther King did not die for Blacks to become pimps, bitches, druggies, and hos. In general, Black ancestors held a strong faith and relationship with God, just like the Israelites. Reconnecting with the Most High is the first thing we need to do. The Israelites even complained about the struggles they faced once they were out of Egypt and expressed their desire to go back to the land of the Israelites, despite how God used Moses and other leaders to bring them out. We cannot forget our beginnings—*big* or *small*; we cannot burn the bridges that brought us across the thresholds to where we are today.[180] But I believe there is hope for young Black and White America.

Steps to Begin to Make Progress

Nannie Helen Burroughs wrote "Twelve Things the Negro Must Do for Himself" circa early 1900's. Change takes time and a gestational period is needed because it is a step-by-step process. Burroughs posits that

> The Negro must learn to put first things first [which] are: education, development of character traits, a trade, and home ownership. The Negro puts too much of his earning in clothes, in food, in show and in having what he calls 'a good time'; '... The Negro buys what he WANTS and begs for what he needs.'[181]

While discrimination is an incubus that has haunted the U.S. since its inception, we must begin to revisit and/or reevaluate our perspectives on education, development of character traits, a trade, and home ownership.

Focusing on education, consider this question: why do some African Americans become interested in education, community, a trade, and setting goals when they are incarcerated? Some prison systems across the U.S. provide inmates an opportunity to attend college, read books, and learn a trade to benefit their life outside bars. We have to begin to take partial responsibility for what our children see and hear in the media. Chuck D posits that "right now [hip-hop] is being used in a way that's negative to the existence of Black people. Jails are being built and they're being filled with nothing but more and more Black people. Black youth under the age of twenty-one are dying at a rapid rate from shooting each other I mean at the ages of nine, ten, eleven, just shooting each other trying to emulate what they see on TV and some [hip-hop] videos."[182] Black masculinity is modeled after what hip-hop artists demonstrate in videos. All youth are impressionable and subject to following the example of their idols—wayward or not.

In addition, our communities are often stereotypic. If we are not in the 'hood', we are on the basketball court, football field, telling jokes, spending money on liquor and then saying "we can't pay the light bill." Our youth are killing each other on the street for street dominance, which only lands them in prison, where they begin to realize that if someone cared about them enough to take them off the streets and put them in programs, served as their mentor, provided discipline and love, then they would have been guided on a more optimistic path.

The second thing we can do—per the advice, Nannie Helen Burroughs—is wipe out mass ignorance on a high resolve. Hip-hop executives, artists, producers, and affiliates are empowered to teach "the masses to become eager and determined to improve mentally, morally, and spiritually."[183] It is hard for me to believe that EVERY hip-hop artist now and in the future will come from *da ghetto*. There is nothing wrong with being in the ghetto; but there is something wrong in staying in the ghetto generation after generation.

The third thing we can do is begin to reeducate ourselves and then reeducate our children to stop hating ourselves. When people hate who they are, they fail to unite. Further, these "self-haters very often make detrimental statements about themselves, their own physical features, and their own people. Another hallmark of self-haters is that they display these behaviors in front of their own and other people. They are most adept at 'attacking' members of their own group; and they create and/or perpetuate language that speaks to self-hatred."[184]

We cannot depend upon hip-hop music or any other outside medium to teach our children—White, Black, German, Latino, and others—about their history and legacy. Jesse Jackson suggests that hip-hop artists must begin to see the value of civil rights pioneer Martin Luther King and critical theorist W. E. B. DuBois who did the groundwork for us to enjoy the rights and privileges we have today. He adds that hip-hop artists "have the power to lift the entire civilization. That's what we did in the '60s. I mean the laws we changed affect everybody. We changed America. We changed the right to vote, open housing. We changed the world. And that's what these artists must do."[185]

Al Sharpton adds: Dr. Martin Luther King Jr. was the man who did the most to break us out of the shackles of racism, rallied against the heinous war in Vietnam and battled for Blacks to be treated like others, with dignity and respect. And he performed all of his acts under the banner of Christianity. The church was his home base.[186] Islam is doing its part by working in the prisons, streets, poor communities, and education, and they build relationships with young Black men. Jesus spread His message in the streets, prisons, and among poor communities for the physical and spiritual betterment of all His people, even though some of the very people He tried to help killed Him.

The fourth thing we can do is watch hip-hop videos with our children and use these moments to discuss what is being said and done in the video. If parents or caregivers do not take such action, they are tacitly relinquishing their parental responsibilities to those hip-hop artists who don't care about children accessing and watching their soft and hardcore porn videos.

The church can get involved actively instead of making cursory comments about *how young people are going to hell if they don't stop listening to devil* music. Honest conversations about the lyrics, beats, videos, and messages can be presented as part of the teaching process for youth. Since the church has been an active part of the Black family, active conversations about these hip-hop messages can be presented honestly. Before the Civil Rights Movement, Blacks prayed, fasted, and sacrificed as a group. Our churches have become so afraid of the hip-hop generation that they will not take the time to educate the youth who are in their communities. Christians, Muslims, and other religious groups have their shortcomings and vices. It should not prevent these groups to have a discussion about matters affecting the Black community and youth. While it is a matter of debate on whether *flowery* language should be presented in a religious setting, we should not be offended if the talks include language like *ass*, *bitch*, and *screw*, whatever the setting is. We should be offended by how complacent the Black race overall has become with the *racism* that has convinced our Black youth that they are *niggas, bitches, hos,* and *tricks.* It is fine to preach messages of prosperity, but if it is not coupled with instructions on how Blacks can obtain it without degrading the race, then the messages preached should be re-evaluated. If religious institutions are mirroring hip-hop culture, they should re-evaluate their effectiveness with youth.

Michelle Mitchell asserts that there is a new phenomenon among religious institutions in Georgia known as "Pimps in the Pulpit" where men, women and children in Georgia are allegedly pimped in exchange for the dollar. She laments, "I walked out of a mega church in Lithonia two years ago, because the pastor was taking up credit cards in the collection plate!"[187]

The fifth thing we—particularly Black women—can do per the advice of bell hooks is to "not be duped into supporting shit that hurts us under the guise of standing beside our men. If black men are betraying us through acts of male violence, we save ourselves and the [human] race by resisting."[188] The onus is on Black male, females, and the White community to do some grassroots organizing to inform and educate all youth.

The sixth thing we can do is pressure radio and video stations to increase airplay of positive hip-hop artists such as, Talib Kweli, Mos Def, Lauren Hill, Wyclef Jean, Dead Prez, and underground acts along with those currently played.

The seventh thing we can do is consider how hip-hop music has shaped us into who we are and how that shaping influenced our relationship with other people. Some questions we can ask to begin a dialogue are:

1.   How would our ancestors feel about some of the current themes of hip-hop music (i.e. misogyny, explicit sexual images in videos, usage of the term 'nigger', and so on)?

2.   If you are a self-confessed *thug, pimp,* or *gangsta* and the police consistently follow or track you, is that racial profiling?
3.   "We don't even control the so-called hip-hop movement now—it's controlled by Whites. So does that mean that our movement is being led by them?"[189]
4.   What is hip-hop's agenda?
5.   How does hip-hop's agenda reach Blacks and Whites en masse positively to promote social change?
6.   Where is the active political presence of hip-hop artists in the struggle for equality? (Note: There are some great things some hip-hop artists are doing within communities.)
7.   Why are Blacks the only race that denigrates itself yet get offended when someone outside the race denigrates us verbally?
8.   What impact does the Civil Rights Movement have on youth born after 1973? How is that impact demonstrated among them?
9.   What themes from the Civil Rights Movement or Black History are prevalent in hip-hop music today?
10.   What are we doing to eliminate institutional racism that is still pervasive throughout the United States?
11.   What revolution is hip-hop commandeering to annihilate social injustices Blacks and Latinos are still faced with?
12.   What is Blackness? Do Blacks have an identity that is for sale? If we sell our *Blackness* en masse, what will happen to our identity? How will the sale affect those generations of youth that come after us?
13.   How can you love non-consciousness hip-hop that embraces niggas, bitches, 'hos, and tricks and fully love yourself?

14.   How are the hip-hop artists' articulations and treatment of the Black woman distinguishable from White slave owners?

The eighth thing we can do is use hip-hop culture to teach our children concepts that will empower them. *Hip-Hop Harry*, a show on TLC and Discovery Kids network, teaches children about respect, kindness, and team building. Hip-Hop Harry can beatbox, rap, and breakdance.[190]

The ninth thing we can do is to engage our youth in the struggle of Blacks through Black History. We cannot depend upon public school teachers, ministers, media, or any other entity to do the teaching for us. If we do not do it, our children are in danger of learning false definitions of Blackness. Education is a powerful tool. If our children are not given the history to assist them in making sound hip-hop musical choices, their lack of experience will prevent them from differentiating between uplifting and condescending hip-hop music. Their perception of manhood, womanhood, sex, intelligence, and history is subject to be skewed in a negative direction if we depend upon hip-hop videos to teach youth about such issues. Once these negative notions have been embedded in their minds as children, it will be quite difficult for their perspectives to change as adults. For they will teach their children what they have been taught, creating a generational cycle that will eventually destroy one person at a time. I repeat: Our children should be taught that "whatever you do most will be what you do best."[191]

The tenth thing we can do is campaign to record companies that we want to hear more from socially conscious artists like The Coup, Mos Def, Common, and Blackalicous. Their messages overall are socially conscious in theme. If we want other hip-hop artists to articulate similar messages, then we need to become leaders by example, assisting in the effort to create positive messages.

Kunjufu offers the eleventh thing we can do. We can begin a writing campaign where we write letters to the media and politicians about stores selling liquor, cigarettes, and drug paraphernalia to minors; we can write letters to judges asking why crack receives greater punishment than cocaine; and we can write letters to the media and police chiefs letting them know the location of crack houses.[192]

Johnetta Cole and Beverly Guy-Sheftall add that the twelfth thing that we can do is "raise feminist sons and daughters who regard one another as equals rather than as enemies." Further, "gender-progressive African-American men can help to construct healthier, more humane definitions of 'manhood' and 'maleness' than those currently dominating popular culture. They can serve as role models for other men."[193]

What Can Hip-Hop Artists Help To Do

Some hip-hop artists are giving back to the community, yes. But it does not change the fact that some of their lyrics are destructive. Some of the reasons why some hip-hop artists argue that there is nothing destructive about their lyrics or video is 1) it is my right to free speech; 2) if the parents find it offensive they need to prevent their child from watching or listening to it; 3) it is representative of how persons from older generations are disconnected from the music of the new generation; and 4) why fight the Black man for making money; it is for entertainment purposes only. Yes, and so is pornography, which is the reason, I suppose, that it is being pitched to four-year-old kids through some hip-hop music videos.

Like Chuck D from *Public Enemy* "I'm a supporter of both Russell Simmons and Andre Harrell to a degree. They've done some remarkable things in [the hip-hop] industry. At the same time when you rub your nose with the white boys, and you're in a position to make things happen, especially if you're the figurehead of an industry, you should do whatever it takes to make waves and force changes. ... We have a level of Black executives in the business who are silent, and don't say anything to the white boys that made them responsible for the music going out to the community."[194] John McWhorter asserts that

> Given the hip-hop world's reflexive alienation, it's no surprise that its explicit political efforts, such as they are, are hardly progressive. Simmons has founded the 'Hip-Hop Summit Action Network' [HSAN] to bring rap stars and fans together to forge a 'bridge between hip-hop and politics.' But HSAN's policy positions are mostly tired bromides. Sticking with the long-discredited idea that urban schools fail because of inadequate funding from the stingy, racist white establishment, for example, HSAN joined forces with the teachers' union to protest New York mayor Bloomberg's proposed education budget for its supposed lack of generosity. HSAN has also stuck it to President Bush for invading Iraq. And it has vociferously protested the affixing of advisory labels on rap CDs that warn parents about the obscene language inside. Fighting for rappers' rights to obscenity: that's some kind of revolution![195]

The Hip-Hop Summit Action Network is a great platform to discuss how the misogynistic face of hip-hop can be lifted. The hip-hop artists brought to the summits are apolitical.

Sticman of the political rap group Dead Prez adds that "people like Russell Simmons, they running around trying to get people to vote and say that's how you participate in making a difference. But they ain't educating people on how the system works. And to me that's criminal, 'cause just getting people to register and vote is just building a base so candidates can exploit the community.... Voting is just a collective voice. Ain't nothing wrong with a collective voice, but you gotta educate people about the system and how it works so young people is not just thinking, 'I made a difference!' 'Cause that's some bullshit." Kanye West responded: That was one of my main points why I wouldn't want to go to a lot of the [hip-hop] summits. ... It's because I'm supposed to be speaking to 3,000 kids about something that I didn't really know about."[196]

According to the *Black Commentator* in 2004, the local chapter of the National Hip-hop Convention submitted a five-point agenda document to the assembled delegates in Chicago which addressed education, economic justice, criminal justice, health, and human rights.[197] These themes should be made paramount in hip-hop music to empower our youth. Let us work now to create a valid cultural legacy so that our children after us can move closer to experiencing the lifetimes of racial equality that we may never have. It is time that we concern ourselves with the cultural inheritance we will leave our children.

Epilogue

Firstly, I am not on a hip-hop witch hunt. I appreciate certain aspects of hip-hop. Much of hip-hop music prides itself with taking a *keep-it-real* approach in presenting its lyrics and videos that is widely accepted by youth. The tone of this text is not intended to suggest negativity towards hip-hop; it is to suggest that I am taking a similar *keep-it-real* approach that is not popular. I was taught that what is popular is not always right, and what is right is not always popular. If I wrote this text as an ode to the vagina, buttocks, niggas, tricks, ghettoes, jails, and drugs, then I conclude that the tone would not be perceived as negative. Our youth have been socialized into believing the images they see within many of the unconscious videos and imitate what they see in droves. We have to begin a discussion on how these messages impact our children since they will one day become the ancestors of those who come after them. What kind of cultural capital do we wish to leave our children? Our ancestors left us a wealth of cultural capital. I do not wish to see it squandered in the name of what is popular today. Sixty years from now, where will you be and what lessons would you want your children to know? Think about your ancestors who you are a culmination of, and determine what they would want to you do.

Hip-hop artists have made some contributions to communities which often times do not make front-page news. And that may be deliberate since some of these artists must maintain *street credibility* in order to sell records. But slavery lasted nearly 300 years since the popularity of it convinced so many people that it is the right thing to do. They saw it as positive, and the more people supported it, the greater it became. Slavery created generations of people who believed that Blacks should be oppressed. And that was the legacy that early slave owners left to their children, which they passed to their children, and so on. Thanks to our Black and White abolitionists who took a stand against slavery, we are able to have better lives. Their stand was not a popular one, but they took a stand for you and me. If some persons decide not to take a stand against anything (inequality, poverty, sexism, and so on), they are silent supporters of it.

Although there is enough culpability to go around, this text does not seek to take a name-and-blame approach. Black-owned record labels do not control the money-making nexus of hip-hop music, which is distribution, not production. At the time of this writing, we can name a number of hip-hop artists who have record labels like Jay-Z, Puffy, and Jermaine Dupri. But they produce the music; they do not distribute it. They have to go through White-owned distribution companies to get their music out to the masses. Russell Simmons, while successful, did not run Def Jam. Rick Rubin did. So who is controlling hip-hop: Blacks or Whites? Begin to evaluate and analyze what you see and not be too quick to embrace everything that media seeks to dishes out that they call "Black culture."

References

1. Throughout this document, I use some derogatory terminology associated with much of hip-hop music. Such terminology used is NOT a part of my natural vernacular.

2. Bankole, K. (2001). *You left your mind in Africa: Journal observation and essays on African American self-hatred.* West Virginia: Nation House Foundation. (p. 7)

3. Rux, C. (2003). Eminem; The new White Negro. In Greg Tate, editor. *Everything But the Burden: What White People are Taking from Black Culture.* (p. 28).

4. It is not the name of an actually song; it is one that is made up.

5. D. C. and Jah, Y. (1997). *Rap, race, and reality: Fight the power.* New York: Doubleday. (p. 103–23)

6. Lyric from the Ying Yang Twins' *Wait: The Whisper Song.* USA (United States of Atlanta).

7. D. C. and Jah, Y. (1997). *Rap, race, and reality: Fight the power.* New York: Doubleday. (p. 103–23)

8. Martin Luther King

9. Ellison, D. Fight for Your Rights, African-Americans Urged. *Houston Chronicle.* July 3, 2006. www.nationalactionnetwork.net/html/news_archive.html. Retrieved October 28, 2006.

10. Blanchard, K. and Johnson, S. (1982). *The one-minute manager.* New York: Berkley Books. (p. 31).

11. In Google, type "Willie Lynch Letter." Any link mirrors the Letter listed here.

12. Bankole, K. (2001). *You left your mind in Africa: Journal observation and essays on African American self-hatred.* West Virginia: Nation House Foundation. (p. 5).

13. Marx, K. http://www.wisdomquotes.com/cat_history.html.

14.   Shakur, T. *Makaveli.* "White man'z world."
15.   See Boskin, J. (1970). "Sambo." In Gary Nash and Richard Weiss' *The great fear: Race in the mind of America.* New York: Holt, Rinehart and Winston as well as Hans Nathan's *Dan Emmett and the rise of the early Negro minstrelsy.* Oklahoma: Norman, 1962.
16.   The Low Down Jibbs. *The Source.* November 2006. No. 204. (p. 40).
17.   This information was aired January 26, 2007 on Hannity and Colmes with Juan Williams. Fox News.
18.   "Where Hip-Hop Was Born." XXL Magazine. May 2007.
19.   Price, Emmett, III. (2006). *Hip-hop Culture.* California: ABC-CLIO. (p. 22).
20.   Martin Luther King, Jr., Malcolm X, Mary McCloud Bethune, Maxine Waters, Rosa Parks, Fannie Lou Hamer, C. Dolores Tucker, Thurgood Marshall, Jesse Jackson, Frank Johnson, Andrew Goodman, Michael Schwerner, and Al Sharpton.
21.   Cepeda, R. "Where is the hip-hop agenda?" *Essence.* Aug. 2000, Vol. 31 Issue 4, p. 117.
22.   D. C. and Jah, Y. (1997). *Rap, race, and reality: Fight the power.* New York: Doubleday. (p. 126).
23.   Martinez, T. (1997). Popular Culture as Oppositional Culture: Rap as Resistance. *Sociological Perspectives* 40: 2, 265–86.
24.   DBrad. *Confessions of a BET Producer. www.myspace.com.*
25.   In *Beef II.* (2004). QD3 Entertainment.
26.   Wiltz, T. and Johnson, D. "The Imus test: Rap lyrics undergo examination." *The Washington Post.* April 25, 2007. (pg. C 1).
27.   Amber, J. "Dirty Dancing." *Essence.* March 2005 (p. 164).
28.   Kitwana, B. (2005). Why White Kids Love Hip-hop. New York: Basic Civitas. (p. 149).
29.   D. C. and Jah, Y. (1997). *Rap , race, and reality: Fight the power.* New York: Doubleday.
30.   Kitwana, B. *Why White Kids Love Hip-Hop.* New York: Basic Civitas. (p. 154–155).
31.   Trivino, J. "Off on a tangent with Ja Rule." *The Hip-Hop Source.* Accessed December 3, 2003. www.sohh.com/thecore/read.php?contentID=5306&pageID=3.
32.   hooks, b. "Sexism and Misogyny." *Z Magazine.* (February 1994). http://race.eserver.org/misogyny.html.
33.   Frosch, D. XXX-Posure. *Vibe: The Sexy Issue.* July 2004. (p. 100 and 103).

34.   Loewenberg, P. *The Pyschology* [sic] *of racism*. In Gary B. Nash and Richard Weiss (Eds). *The Great Fear: Race in the mind of America*. (1970). Chicago: Holt, Rinehart, and Winston. (p. 192).

35.   Evelyn, J. "The miseducation of hip-hop." *Black Issues in Higher Education*. Vol. 17, Issue 21, p. 24.

36.   Staples, B. as cited by Tiambi Barnes in "Off the Cuff." *The Source*. December 2005, No. 194. (p. 76).

37.   Allah, D. "Prison Industry/Music Industry." *The Source*. December 2005, No. 194. (p. 26).

38.   Intelligent, W. Who the Hell am I? Has Jay-Z Outgrown Hip-Hop? An Intelligent Response. *Davey D's Hip-hop Blog*. Friday, December 8, 2006. blog.myspace.com/mrdaveyd. Retrieved December 28, 2006.

39.   Barrow, Jerry. Instinctive Travels. *The Source*. June 2005. No.188. (p. 93). Interview with Mos Def.

40.   The acronym, KRS-One, stands for Knowledge Reigns Supreme Over Nearly Everyone.

41.   Slaughter, Peter. *Barutiwa Weekly News*. 7 June 1997. Volume 1, Issue 4.

42.   As cited in Mills, K. (1993). *This little light of mine: The life of Fannie Lou Hamer*. New York: Plume. (p. 60).

43.   King, M. L. Jr. http://www.brainyquote.com/quotes/authors/m/ martin_luther_king_jr.html.

44.   McChesney, Robert. Global Bits—Creating Culture—Young People and Advertising. Issue 3. 2004. Global Education Centre. http://www. globaled.org.nz.

45.   Blake, Reynard. Dismantling the 'Bling': Another Look at Hip-Hop. *The Black Commentator*. Issue 99. July 15, 2004.

46.   Kunjufu, J. (2005). *Hip-hop street curriculum: Keeping it real*. Chicago: African American Images. (p. 127).

47.   Hutchinson, E. (1996). *The Assassination of the Black Male Image*. New York: Touchstone. (p. 143–144).

48.   Kitwana, B. (2002). *The hip-hop generation: Young Blacks and the Crisis in African-American culture*. New York: Basic Civitas. p. 6–8.

49.   Bowling, D. "Young, gifted, and Wack." Retrieved December 18, 2003. http://www.msnbc.msn.com/id/3677687.

50.   Research Staff of National Vanguard Books. *Who Rules America? The Alien Grip on Our News and Entertainment Media Must be Broken*. Retrieved 10/28/2006. http://server8.iicinternet.com/wcotc/ritualmord/ id189_m.htm.

51.   Barrow, Jerry. Instinctive Travels. *The Source*. June 2005. No.188. (p. 93). Interview with Mos Def.

52. Irvin, a Wake Forest professor as cited in Evelyn, J. "The miseducation of hip-hop." *Black Issues in Higher Education*. Vol. 17, Issue 21, p. 24.

53. Trivino, J. "Off on a targent with Ja Rule." *The Hip-Hop Source*. Accessed December 3, 2003. www.sohh.com/thecore/read. php?contentID=5306&pageID=3.

54. *Hip-hop Generation Agenda: More than Music and Style*. The Black Commentator. Issue 97, July 1, 2004. http://www.blackcommentator. com/97/97_cover_hh_convention_pf.html.

55. *Hip-hop Generation Agenda: More than Music and Style*. The Black Commentator. Issue 97, July 1, 2004. http://www.blackcommentator. com/97/97_cover_hh_convention_pf.html.

56. Holley, S. as cited by Rob "biko" Baker in "Just to Get a Rep." *The Source*. December 2005, No. 194. (p. 41).

57. Mike. "Hip-Hop Behind Bars: Dear Hip-Hop." *The Source*. December 2005, No. 194. (p. 100).

58. Kirkland, R. as cited in Allah, M. "The 'Hood's Hoop Prophet." *The Source*. December 2005, No. 194. (p. 117).

59. Freire, P. (1993). *Pedagogy of the Oppressed*. New York: The Continuum Publishing Company. (p. 44).

60. Wingood, G. et al. A Prospective Study of Exposure to Rap Music Videos and African American Female Adolescents' Health. *American Journal of Public Health*. 2003 March 93(3): 437–439.

61. hooks, b. "Sexism and Misogyny." *Z Magazine*. (February 1994). http:// race.eserver.org/misogyny.html.

62. Loewenberg, P. (1970). "The Psychology of Racism." In Gary Weiss and Gary Nash's *The Great fear: Race in the Mind of America*. New York: Holt, Rinehart, and Winston. (p. 193).

63. Woodson, C. (1990). *The Mis-Education of the Negro*. New Jersey: Africa World Press. 11th Printing. (p. xii).

64. www.cliffnotes.com/WileyCDA/LitNote/id84,pageNum-54.html.

65. D. C. and Jah, Y. (1997). *Rap, race, and reality: Fight the power*. New York: Doubleday. (p. 6).

66. Kelley, N. "The Political Economy of Black Music." *Black Renaissance/ Renaissance Noire*. Summer 1999. http://www.hartford-hwp.com/ archives/45a/358.html. Retrieved September 27, 2002.

67. D. C. and Jah, Y. (1997). *Rap, race, and reality: Fight the power*. New York: Doubleday. (p. 46).

68. Gibbs, M. (2003). In Greg Tate, editor. *Everything But the Burden: What White People are Taking from Black Culture*. (p. 82).

69. Hutchinson, E. (1996). *Assassination of the Black Male Image*. New York: Touchstone. (p. 28). Hutchinson cites Michael L. Radelet. Execution of

Whites for Crimes Against Blacks: Exceptions to the Rule? *Sociological Quarterly,* Vol. 30, 1989, 529–44.

70.   As quote in Earl Ofari Hutchinson's (1997). *The assassination of the black male image.* New York: Touchstone.

71.   Hurst, H. Reality Theater: A Real Nigga Show. *The Baltimore Afro-American.* July 23, 2005–July 29, 2005. A4–A5.

72.   Dave Chappelle. February 3, 2006. *Oprah.*

73.   Davey D. *Nigga or Nigger.* www.daveyd.com/nigaornigpol.html. Retrieved December 3, 2003.

74.   Waldron, C. "After Imus: Black Champion Women, Civility and Decency. *Jet.* April 20, 2007.

75.   Tate, G. (2003). Introduction. *Everything But the Burden: What White People are Taking from Black Culture.* New York: Broadway Books. (p. 8).

76.   Scott, Paul. *Who Speaks for 'Tha Nigga'?* http://pub12.ezboard.com. Retrieved December 3, 2003.

77.   Lucas, D. Ear to the Street: Shock and Awe. *The Source.* No. 204. (p. 24).

78.   Frosch, D. XXX-Posure. *Vibe: The Sexy Issue.* July 2004. (p. 102).

79.   D'Ambrosio, A. Chuck D. Interview. *The Progressive.* http://www.progressive.org/?q=notde/2191. retrieved October 28, 2006. (from the August 2005 issue).

80.   hooks, b. "Sexism and Misogyny." *Z Magazine.* (February 1994). http://race.eserver.org/misogyny.html.

81.   hooks, bell. Misogyny, Gangsta Rap, and The Piano. *Z-Magazine.* March 4, 1994.

82.   Douglass, F. (1962). *Life and Times of Frederick Douglass.* New York: Collier Books.

83.   D'Ambrosio, A. Chuck D. Interview. *The Progressive.* http://www.progressive.org/?q=notde/2191. retrieved October 28, 2006. (from the August 2005 issue).

84.   Van Silk, "Straight from the Source?" (26 Jan. 2003). <http://www.extremekicks.com/vansilk/whatishiphop.html>. par. 13.

85.   As told to Clover Hope in "Whatz Next?" In *XXL Magazine.* May 2007.

86.   D'Ambrosio, A. Chuck D. Interview. *The Progressive.* http://www.progressive.org/?q=notde/2191. retrieved October 28, 2006. (from the August 2005 issue).

87.   Roberts, J. "The rap of luxury." *Newsweek.* (September 2, 2002). (p. 42).

88.   Kunjufu, J. (2005). *Hip-hop street curriculum: Keeping it real.* Chicago: African American Images.

89.   hooks, b. "Sexism and Misogyny." *Z Magazine.* (February 1994). http://race.eserver.org/misogyny.html.

90.   McHorter, J. (2000). *Losing the race.* New York: The Free Press.

91. Kitwana, B. (2002). *Young Blacks and the Crisis in African-American Culture: The Hip-Hop Generation.* New York: Basic Civitas Books. (p. 73).

92. Kunjufu, J. (2005). *Hip-hop street curriculum: Keeping it real.* Chicago: African American Images. (p. 48).

93. Kitwana, B. (2002). *Young Blacks and the Crisis in African-American Culture: The Hip-Hop Generation.* New York: Basic Civitas Books. (p. 73).

94. This name is a pseudonym to protect the identity of the person who shared this information with me.

95. Mariner, Joanne. *FindLaw.* As cited in Mass Incarceration and Rape: The Savaging of Black America. *The Black Commentator.* Issue 95. June 17, 2004. www.blackcommentator.com/95/95_cover_prisons_pf.html. Retrieved December 31, 2006.

96. Kunjufu, J. (2005). *Hip-hop street curriculum: Keeping it real.* Chicago: African American Images.

97. Lucas, D. What they forgot to tell you. *Hip-Hop Music, Culture, & Politics.* March 2007. (p. 208).

98. Matthews, A. "Keep Me Down." *XXL Magazine.* (July 2005).No. 71. (p. 56).

99. *XXL Magazine.* (July 2005). No. 71. (p. 82).

100. *XXL Magazine.* (July 2005). No. 71. (p. 84).

101. *XXL Magazine.* (July 2005). No. 71. (p. 94).

102. Kunjufu, J. (2005). *Hip-hop street curriculum: Keeping it real.* Chicago: African American Images. (p. 76–77).

103. Stoltenberg, J. "Pornography and Freedom" in *Men's lives,* ed. Michael S. Kimmel and Michael A. Messner. New York: MacMillan 1989. (p. 482–488).

104. Loewenberg, P. In Gary Nash and Richard Weiss' *The great fear: Race in the mind of America.* (1970). New York: Holt, Rinehart, and Winston.

105. This quote is found in *Essence.* August 8, 2004. Taigi Smith is the author of the part-two report on "Deadly Deception."

106. This information was shared with me by a former college student of mine in discussing what he witnessed in prison. His name has been changed to protect his identity.

107. Stephen Donaldson. Excerpts from a lecture delivered at Columbia University on February 4, 1993. It is found in Don Sabo, Terry Kupers, and Willie London (2001) (eds) *Prison Masculinities.* Philadelphia: Temple University Press.

108. Stephen Donaldson. Excerpts from a lecture delivered at Columbia University on February 4, 1993. It is found in Don Sabo, Terry Kupers,

and Willie London (2001) (eds) *Prison Masculinities*. Philadelphia: Temple University Press.

109.   Stephen Donaldson. Excerpts from a lecture delivered at Columbia University on February 4, 1993. It is found in Don Sabo, Terry Kupers, and Willie London (2001) (eds) *Prison Masculinities*. Philadelphia: Temple University Press.

110.   Whitlock, J. Hip-hop Serving Up Plan for Failure Black Youth Need to Break Free of Prison Culture. www.aol.com. Retrieved May 6, 2007.

111.   Thompson, B. "Knowledge Me." *XXL Magazine*. (July 2005). (p. 55).

112.   The Game. *High Times*. June 2005. as cited in XXL. "Negro Please." July 2005, No. 71. (p. 46).

113.   TMZ.com. http://www.tmz.com/2006/11/21/snoop-blunt-smokeperson. retrieved November 21, 2006.

114.   Kunjufu, J. (2005). *Hip-hop street curriculum: Keeping it real*. Chicago: African American Images. (p. 51).

115.   D. C. and Jah, Y. (1997). *Rap, Race, and Reality: Fight the Power*. New York: Doubleday. (p. 251).

116.   Blake, Reynard. Dismantling the 'Bling': Another Look at Hip-Hop. *The Black Commentator*. Issue 99. July 15, 2004.

117.   Tate, G. (2003). Introduction. *Everything But the Burden: What White People are Taking from Black Culture*. New York: Broadway Books. (p. 12).

118.   Freire, P. (1993). *Pedagogy of the Oppressed*. New York: The Continuum Publishing Company. (p. 40).

119.   Freire, P. *Pedagogy of the Oppressed*. New York: The Continuum Publishing Company. (p. 37).

120.   D. C. and Jah, Y. (1997). *Rap, Race, and Reality: Fight the Power*. New York: Doubleday. (p. 31).

121.   D. C. and Jah, Y. (1997). *Rap, Race, and Reality: Fight the Power*. New York: Doubleday. (p. 33).

122.   D. C. and Jah, Y. (1997). *Rap, Race, and Reality: Fight the Power*. New York: Doubleday. (p. 186).

123.   Hopkins, J. Hip-hop Music Raising a Tragic Crop of Teen Age Pimps and Prostitutes. *Pasadena Journal*. Editorial, February 12, 2004. www. pasadenajournal.com/id61.html. Retrieved October 28, 2006.

124.   Kunjufu, J. (2005). *Hip-hop street curriculum: Keeping it real*. Chicago: African American Images.

125.   Barrow, Jerry. Instinctive Travels. *The Source*. June 2005. No.188. (p. 90). Interview with Mos Def.

126.   D. C. and Jah, Y. (1997). *Rap, Race, and Reality: Fight the Power*. New York: Doubleday. (p. 259).

127.   *XXL.* "Still on it: Mixtapes might be dying, but beef never will." May 2007.

128.   *Tupac resurrection: In his own words.* (2003). MTV/Films Amaru Entertainment.

129.   *Tupac resurrection: In his own words.* (2003). MTV/Films Amaru Entertainment.

130.   This chart was extracted from www.en.wikipedia.org/East_Coast-West_Coast_hip_hop_rivalry. Retrieved July 12, 2007.

131.   *Hip-hop Generation Agenda: More than Music and Style.* The Black Commentator. Issue 97, July 1, 2004. http://www.blackcommentator.com/97/97_cover_hh_convention_pf.html.

132.   It is part of Nelly's song *Tip Drill.*

133.   Johnson, A. (1997). *The gender knot: Unraveling our patriarchal legacy.* Philadelphia: Temple University Press. (p. 39).

134.   The Best and Worst of 2006: Say What? *Essence.* December 2006. (p. 72).

135.   *Cultural Criticism and Transformation.* bell hooks video. (Media Educational Foundation, 1996).

136.   Amott, T. and Julie Matthaei. (1996). *Race, gender, and work: A multi-cultural economic history of women in the United States.* Boston: South End Press.

137.   Amott, T. and Julie Matthaei. (1996). *Race, gender, and work: A multi-cultural economic history of women in the United States.* Boston: South End Press.

138.   As cited in Amott, T. and Julie Matthaei. (1996). *Race, gender, and work: A multi-cultural economic history of women in the United States.* Boston: South End Press.

139.   Hutchinson, E. (1996). *The Assassination of the Black Male Image.* New York: Touchstone. (p. 16–17)

140.   Loewenberg, P. The Pyschology [sic] of racism. In Gary B. Nash and Richard Weiss (Eds). *The Great Fear: Race in the mind of America.* (1970). Chicago: Holt, Rinehart, and Winston. (p.194).

141.   Oh Say Can You See?: Why Pornography is Our *Real* National Pastime. *Vibe.* July 2004. (p.101).

142.   Slaughter, *Barutiwa Weekly.* 7 June 1997.

143.   "From Violent Video Games to Condoms and Sex Toys: Is 50 Cent Doin' Too Much? *The Challenger.* Vol. 42, No. 46.

144.   Amber, J. "Dirty Dancing." *Essence.* March 2005 (p. 164).

145.   Stephens, K. (2005). *Confessions of a Video Vixen.* New York: Amistad. (p. xiii).

146.   Johnson, A. (1997). *The gender knot: Unraveling our patriarchical legacy.* Philadelphia: Temple University Press. (p. 173).

147.   Amber, J. "Dirty Dancing." *Essence*. March 2005 (p. 165).

148.   Amber, J. "Dirty Dancing." *Essence*. March 2005 (p. 165)

149.   Hopkinson, N. and Moore, N. (2006). *Deconstructing Tyrone: A New Look at Black Masculinity in the Hip-Hop Generation*. California: Cleis Press. (p. 90).

150.   Loewenberg, P. *The Pyschology* [sic] *of racism*. In Gary B. Nash and Richard Weiss (Eds). *The Great Fear: Race in the mind of America*. (1970). Chicago: Holt, Rinehart, and Winston. (p. 196).

151.   Loewenberg, P. *The Pyschology* [sic] *of racism*. In Gary B. Nash and Richard Weiss (Eds). *The Great Fear: Race in the mind of America*. (1970). Chicago: Holt, Rinehart, and Winston. (p. 198).

152.   Hugo Schwyzer talks about it based upon Michael Kimmel's explanation of homosociality in Manhood in America.

153.   Hugo Schwyzer talks about it based upon Michael Kimmel's explanation of homosociality in Manhood in America.

154.   Hopkinson, N. and Moore, N. (2006). *Deconstructing Tyrone: A New Look at Black Masculinity in the Hip-Hop Generation*. California: Cleis Press. (p. 86).

155.   Lerner, Gerda. Ed. (1972). *Black Women in White America*. New York: Pantheon Books. (p. 216)

156.   Hutchinson, E. (1996). *Assassination of the Black Male Image*. New York: Touchstone. (p. 173).

157.   Hutchinson, E. (1996). *Assassination of the Black Male Image*. New York: Touchstone. (p. 66).

158.   Covington, J. "Self-esteem and deviance: The effects of race and gender." *Crimnology* 24. November 1986. 105–138.

159.   D. C. and Jah, Y. (1997). *Rap, race, and reality: Fight the power*. New York: Doubleday. (p. 104).

160.   White, John. (1985). *Black Leadership in America: 1895-1968*. New York: Longman, 1985.

161.   Blake, Reynard. Dismantling the 'Bling': Another Look at Hip-Hop. *The Black Commentator*. Issue 99. July 15, 2004.

162.   Amber, J. "Dirty Dancing." *Essence*. March 2005. (p. 166 and 203)

163.   Edlund, M. *Hip-hop's crossover to the adult aisle*. March 7, 2004. Retrieved March 10, 2004. http://www.nytimes.com/2004/03/07/arts/music/07EDLU.html.

164.   Stephens, K. (2005). *Confessions of a Video Vixen*. New York: Amistad. (p. 209).

165.   Bowling, D. "Young, gifted, and Wack." Retrieved December 18, 2003. http://www.msnbc.msn.com/id/3677687.

166.   Freire, P. (1993). *Pedagogy of the Oppressed*. New York: Continuum Publishing Company. (p. 44).

167.   Freire, P. (1993). *Pedagogy of the Oppressed*. New York: Continuum Publishing Company. (p. 55)

168.   Barrow, Jerry. Instinctive Travels. *The Source*. June 2005. No.188. (p. 90). Interview with Mos Def.

169.   Kunjufu, J. (2005). *Hip-hop street curriculum: Keeping it real*. Chicago: African American Images. (p. 35).

170.   Lewis, G. Craig. Ex Ministries: The truth behind hip-hop. Fort Worth, TX 76124.

171.   Stephens, K. (2005). *Confessions of a Video Vixen*. New York: Amistad. (p. 209).

172.   Maya Angelou.

173.   Amerikaz Nightmare. Produced by Vanessa Satten and Bonsu Thompson. Moderated by Dave Chappelle. *XXL Magazine*. October 2004. (p. 134).

174.   www.allhip.com/hiphopnews/?ID=6472. Retrieved December 29, 2006.

175.   www.allhip.com/hiphopnews/?ID=6472. Retrieved December 29, 2006.

176.   Bankole, K. (2001). *You left your mind in Africa: Journal observations and essays on African-American self-hatred*. Dellslow, WV: Nation House Foundation.

177.   Bishop Robert Taylor, Fellowship Tabernacle Church, Statesville, NC. Telephone conversation on December 29, 2006.

178.   Dake's Annotated Reference Bible. (1963). Exodus Chapter One versus 7–22. Bishop Robert Taylor, Fellowship Tabernacle Church, Statesville, NC directed me to this book, chapter, and verse via telephone conversation on December 29, 2006.

179.   Nelly. *Tip Drill* lyrics.

180.   Bishop Robert Taylor, Fellowship Tabernacle Church, Statesville, NC. Telephone conversation on December 29, 2006.

181.   Burroughs, N. H. "Twelve things the Negro must do for himself." Retrieved November 21, 2006 from http://d01.webmail.aol.com/22250/aol/en-us/Mail/display-message-body.aspx?

182.   D. C. and Jah, Y. (1997). *Rap, race, and reality: Fight the power*. New York: Doubleday. (p. 254)

183.   Burroughs, N. H. "Twelve things the Negro must do for himself." Retrieved November 21, 2006 from http://d01.webmail.aol.com/22250/aol/en-us/Mail/display-message-body.aspx?

184.   Bankole, K. (2001). *You left your mind in Africa: Journal observation and essays on African American self-hatred*. West Virginia: Nation House Foundation. (p. 21).

185. Saunders, Warner. Since Hip-Hop Beat-Boxed Black America and the Rest of the World: Five Views. *Savoy.* February 2005. (p. 31).

186. National Action Network. *Commentary: Sexually-Based Issues Dividing Black Churches by Rev. Al Sharpton.* Special to CNN. July 6, 2006. www. nationalactionnetwork.net/html/news_archive.html. Retrieved October 28, 2006.

187. Mitchell, M. "Are we carrying around baggage of Black codes?" *The Black Commentator.* April 19, 2007. Issue 226.

188. hooks, b. "Sexism and Misogyny." *Z Magazine.* (February 1994). http:// race.eserver.org/misogyny.html

189. Iverem, E. In Artelia Covington's *Has Hip-hop Replaced the Civil Rights Movement?* http://www.blackpressusa.com/news/Article.asp. Retrieved October 28, 2006.

190. Take 'Em to School: New Show Uses Hip-Hop Culture to Teach Kids. *The Source.* November 2006. No. 204. (p. 32).

191. Kunjufu, J. (2005). *Hip-hop street curriculum: Keeping it real.* Chicago: African American Images. (p. 127)

192. Kunjufu, J. (2005). *Hip-hop street curriculum: Keeping it real.* Chicago: African American Images. (p. 127)

193. Cole, J. and Guy-Sheftall, B. (2003). *Gender talk: The struggle for women's equality in African American communities.* New York: One World. (p. 220–221).

194. D. C. and Jah, Y. (1997). *Rap, race, and reality: Fight the power.* New York: Doubleday. (p. 126).

195. McWhorter, J. "How hip-hop holds Blacks back." *City Journal.* Summer 2003.

196. Amerikaz Nightmare. Produced by Vanessa Satten and Bonsu Thompson. Moderated by Dave Chappelle. XXL Magazine. October 2004. (p. 128).

197. *Hip-hop Generation Agenda: More than Music and Style.* The Black Commentator. Issue 97, July 1, 2004. http://www.blackcommentator. com/97/97_cover_hh_convention_pf.html.

Index

Printed in the United States
212339BV00004B/6/P

9 781934 269510